Leonardo da Vinci
by James Pearson

Early Netherlandish Painting
by Rosalind Mutter

Piero della Francesca
by Naomi Haskell

Giovanni Bellini
by Julia Davis

Eric Gill: Nuptials of God
by Anthony Hoyland

Minimal Art and Artists In the 1960s and After
by Laura Garrard

Postwar Art
by George Knighton

Vincent van Gogh: Visionary Landscapes
by Stuart Morris

Max Beckmann
by Stuart Morris

Egon Schiele: Sex and Death in Purple Stockings
by D. Simon Eade

Mark Rothko: The Art of Transcendence
by Julia Davis

Jasper Johns
by L.M. Poole

Brice Marden
by Laura Garrard

Frank Stella: American Abstract Artist
by James Pearson

The Light Eternal: J.M.W. Turner
by Jeremy Mark Robinson

Maurice Sendak and the Art of Children's Book Illustration
by L.M. Poole

Sex in Art: Pornography and Pleasure in Painting and Sculpture
by Cassidy Hughes

*Glorification: Religious Abstraction
In Renaissance and 20th Century Painting*
by Jeremy Mark Robinson

The Art of Andy Goldsworthy
by William Malpas

Andy Goldsworthy: Touching Nature
by William Malpas

Andy Goldsworthy In Close-Up
by William Malpas

The Art of Richard Long
by William Malpas

Constantin Brancusi: Sculpting the Essence of Things
by James Pearson

Alison Wilding: The Embrace of Sculpture
by Susan Quinnell

*The Erotic Object: Sexuality in Sculpture
From Prehistory to the Present Day*
by Susan Quinnell

*Land Art: A Complete Guide to Landscape, Environmental,
Earthworks, Nature, Sculpture and Installation Art*
by William Malpas

Land Art In Close-Up
by William Malpas

*Colourfield Painting: Minimal, Cool, Hard Edge, Serial
and Post-Painterly Abstract Art From the Sixties to the Present*
by Laura Garrard

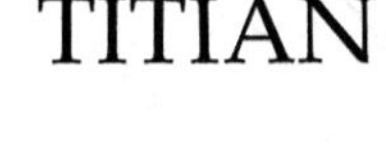

TITIAN

TITIAN

S.L. BENSUSAN

CRESCENT MOON

First published 1908. This edition © 2017.

Printed and bound in the U.S.A.
Set in Book Antiqua 10 on 14pt.
Designed by Radiance Graphics.

Thanks to the authors and publishers quoted.

British Library Cataloguing in Publication data

ISBN-13 9781861716095(Pbk)

CRESCENT MOON PUBLISHING
P.O. Box 1312, Maidstone, Kent, ME14 5XU
Great Britain, www.crmoon.com

CONTENTS

NOTE ON THE TEXT

The text is from *Titian* by S.L. Bensusan, published by T.C. &
E.C. Jack, London and Frederick A. Stokes, New York, 1908, as
part of the Masterpieces In Colour series, edited by T. Leman
Hare.

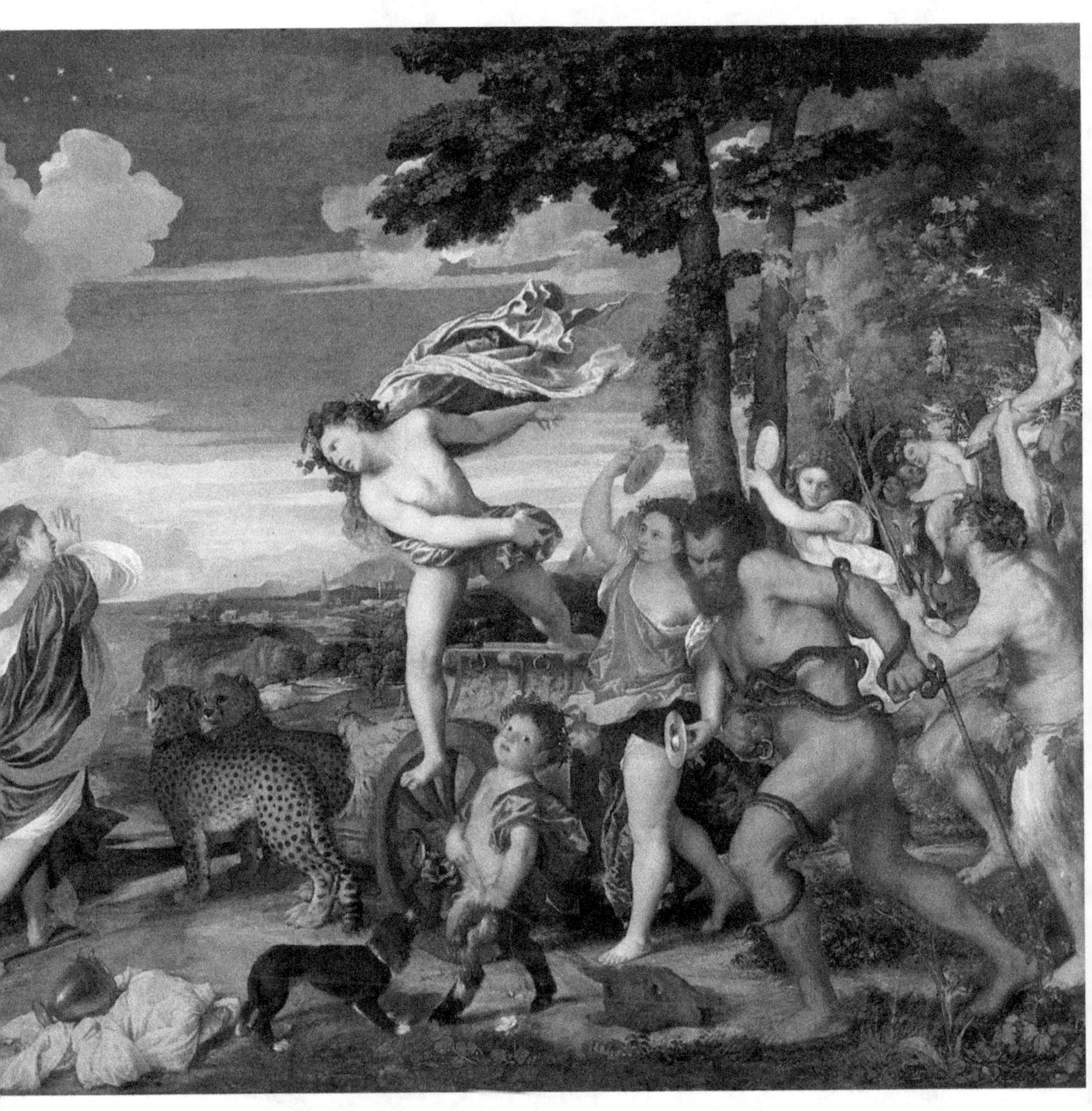

Titian, Bacchus and Ariadne, 1520-23, London

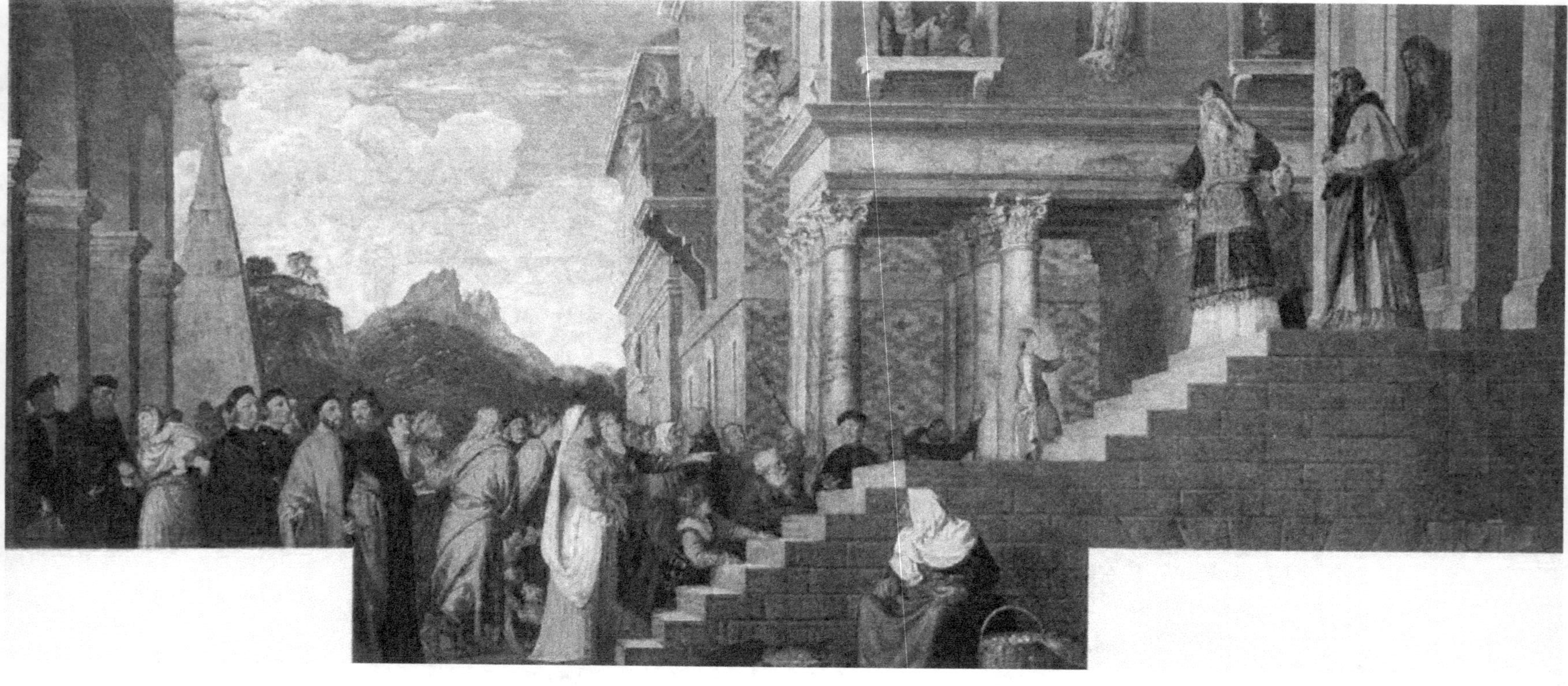

Titian, The Presentation of the Virgin, 1534-38

I

TITAN

Titian Vecelli, undeniably the greatest Venetian painter of the Renaissance, leaps into the full light of the movement. To be sure he appears full-grown, as Venus is said to have done when she appeared above the foam in the waters of Cythera, or Pallas Athene when she sprang from the brain of Zeus, but happily he was destined to live to a great age.

We have few and scanty records to tell of the very early days. So wide was his circle of patrons in after life, so intimate his acquaintance with the leading men of his generation, that it is not difficult to find out what manner of man he was without the aid of his pictures, even though they have a very definite story to tell the painstaking student.

There are well over one hundred important works, dealing with the life and art of Titian, written by enthusiasts in half-a-dozen languages, for of all the artists of the Renaissance he makes perhaps the most direct appeal to the man *moyen sensuel*.

Fearless and unashamed, he gave the world pagan pictures, entering into the joy of their creation with the enthusiasm of a schoolboy who has found an orchard gate unlocked. To be sure the spirit of joy and of youth passed with the years, even this most fortunate of painters knew trouble, domestic and financial, but the beauty remained, expressing the fullest vigour of the Renaissance movement, the supreme achievement of human loveliness, the splendour of men and women.

Fortune was kind to Titian in many ways, and not in the least degree by driving to the sheltering fold of the Venetian Republic the great men of all lands who were hurrying to safety before the destroying advance of Spain. It is right, at the same time, to remember that the leaders of the destroying legions were the friends and patrons of the painter, that the greatest of them all desired to be buried in the shadow of the master's picture "La Gloria," now in the Prado. The time called for a supremely gifted artist to render its great men immortal, or at least to give them what we call immortality in the days when we forget that if modern science be correct man has existed for some 250,000 years and has not yet reached mental adolescence. Perhaps when he has developed his brain, and can control the march of this planet and the duration of his own life, he will not make half so attractive a subject for the painters as did those men and women of the fifteenth and sixteenth century whose beauty casts a spell over us to-day.

Titian was born at Pieve among the mountains of Cadore where the Tyrol and Italy meet. His statue in bronze looks out towards Venice to-day from the market-place of his native town, and the landscape that the painter knew best, and gave time out of mind to his pictures, has altered but little. He was a second son, and would seem to have been born about the year 1480, but there was no registrar of births, marriages, and deaths in Pieve and, while some authorities place the date at 1477, the year that he himself favoured, others advance it as far as 1482. There has been a great controversy about this birth date, but it might be safe to place it rather later still.

Titian was the son of one Gregorio Vecelli, who seems to have been a soldier and a man who held high position in the little town which, in the early days of the fifteenth century, had cast in its lot with the Venetian Republic. Nothing is known of his mother except her name, but his elder brother named Francesco followed art until he was middle aged, and there were two sisters Ursula and Katherine, of whom the former kept house for the painter for many years in Venice, after the death of his wife.

Francesco and Titian Vecelli developed at an early age a marked feeling for painting, and in order that they might have every chance of developing their gifts to the best advantage, Gregorio Vecelli took them to Venice, which lay some seventy miles from Pieve, and left them with a brother who had sufficient influence to secure for Titian admission to the studios of the brothers Bellini, who then shared with the Vivarini family the highest position in the art world of the Republic. Gian Bellini, then a man past middle age, had in his studio several pupils who were destined to achieve distinction. Palma Vecchio, Sebastian del Piombo, and Giorgione of Castelfranco were among them, and of these the last named was certainly the greatest. It is probable that, had he lived, even Titian Vecelli must have toiled after him in vain, for he influenced his fellow-student to an extent that is very clearly revealed in the early pictures, and has even led to confusion between the work of the two men, a confusion greatly increased by the fact that Titian completed some of the pictures that Giorgione left unfinished. Happily perhaps for Titian, though unfortunately for the world at large, Giorgione was destined to fall a victim to one of the plagues that ravaged Venice from time to time, and he died soon after completing his thirtieth year, leaving Titian undisputed master of Venetian painting.

Like all great men Titian was an assimilator. In his early days he started out under the influence of Bellini. Then he surrendered, as even his aged master did, to the strange, rare, and beautiful spirit of poetry and romance that Giorgione brought into art. He may have helped to develop and strengthen it, for he and Giorgione worked and lived together. Finally when outside influences had died down Titian found himself, and this was the greatest discovery of his life.

In the last years of Giorgione's short career he and Titian, both young men, were engaged to decorate the great Commercial House of the Germans, rebuilt upon the site of the older building that had been destroyed by fire about the beginning of the year 1505. The work would appear to have been started two years later. This united effort, purely decorative, must have been worthy of its surroundings at a time when Venice and beauty were almost synonymous terms; the greater part is lost to us to-day.

Serious troubles were upon the Republic. The League of Cambrai, one of the least scrupulous political arrangements in European history, had resulted in an attack upon the Venetian domains that had been entirely successful, though statecraft was destined to recover from the Philistines of Europe a part at least of what they had taken, and finding that the Republic was too beset to give much thought to art or artists Titian left Venice for Padua. This must have been very shortly after the completion of his work with Giorgione. His hand is to be seen in the very pleasant and learned city of Padua among the frescoes in the Scuola del Santo, and he may have been within its walls when the plague, on one of its periodical visits to Venice, added his friend and fellow-worker Giorgione to a heavy list of victims.

On Titian's return to the headquarters of the Republic only Palma Vecchio was left among the great men of his own age, and it would seem that Titian's rising fame had already spread beyond the borders of Venice, because in 1513, when he petitioned the Council of Ten for a broker's patent to work in the Hall of the German Merchants, he stated that he had been invited by the Pope (Leo X.) to come to Rome, and that he wished to leave a memorial in Venice. It is clear from the correspondence that he had an eye upon a post held by the aged Gian Bellini. This was the office of painter in the Hall of the Great Council, a coveted position for which Carpaccio, one of Bellini's less distinguished pupils, is said to have been among the claimants. Although Titian was a remarkable and rising man the Council hesitated to grant his request, partly because times were bad with the State and money was scarce. He was compelled to wait, and it would appear that his application was opposed both by the friends of Bellini and the supporters of Bellini's older pupils; but as soon as Bellini died, towards the close of 1516, Titian came to his desire and undertook to paint the great battle of Cadore in the Hall of the Great Council. Having secured his patent, work increased, his brush was in request in many quarters, and he did as so many other painters in the State employment of Venice had done – he left his official work for such spare time as more remunerative employment left him – to the great scandal of the Councillors whose angry protests are on record. His early portraits seem to have been of men; the women, in whose treatment he was perhaps less happy, sought him in later life, and his other early commissions were very largely for altar-pieces. Titian had powerful friends and patrons at an early age, for we see that he had been recommended to the Pope by Cardinal Bembo before he returned to Venice from Padua, and his pictures attracted the attention of that splendid patron of art Alfonso of Ferrara. This great connoisseur sent for and entertained him at his castle, and even offered to take him to Rome when Leo X. died, and his successor, after the fashion of Popes, would be likely to give some liberal commissions to the greatest artists of his time. In return for these kindnesses, and in consideration of a splendid fee, Titian painted the great picture of Alfonso of Ferrara of which a copy is to be seen in Florence. The original went to Madrid and has been lost. For the same generous master he painted his "Bacchus and Ariadne," his "Venus with the Shell," and a Bacchanal, and it is generally agreed that he painted a part at least of the picture called "The Bacchanal," now in the possession of the Duke of Northumberland.

Several of the works painted in Ferrara were taken in later days to Madrid, and it might be said in this place that it is almost as necessary to go to the Prado to see the Titians as it is to see the great works of Velazquez. "The Bacchanal" is there, and the

"Worship of Venus" is there, and we find many others of the first importance, some two dozen, perhaps, whose authority is beyond dispute. This collection in the Prado is the more valuable because it represents Titian not only in the early days, but when he was at the zenith of his powers. The pictures range in date over a period of nearly seventy years, from the "Madonna with St. Bridget and St. Ulphus" (circa 1505) down to the "Allegory of the Battle of Lepanto," which was sent to Spain in 1575, a commission from Philip II. whose love for allegorical pictures is well known. Charles V. and his son Philip II. are to be seen in the Prado through the medium of Titian's brush, and, although many of the works have suffered from restoration, which is one of the vices associated with the great Spanish picture galleries, there are several that show few signs of an alien brush and are, for pictures by Titian, in first-class order.

Students of the Renaissance know that art was accepted by all the great rulers of Europe as something lying outside the boundaries of ambition and strife. It was one of the rewards of a great conqueror that he could have his portrait painted by the first painter of his day, and patriotism was kept outside the studio, to the great benefit of art and rulers alike. Venice offended Spain in many ways, and even offended the Church by laying a restraining hand upon the Holy Inquisition, but Popes and Spanish kings were proud, nevertheless, to be numbered among the patrons of the greatest artist of their time, they seemed to know that his brush would do more than immortalise their progress – that it would outlive it. The attention that Titian received from the Court of Ferrara did much to develop the esteem in which Venice held him, and Titian was requested to paint his famous "Assumption" for the great Church of Santa Maria de' Frari. To-day no more than a copy hangs in the church, the picture having been long ago transferred to the Accademia. It is very properly regarded by the authorities as one of the first very great pictures of Titian's life, marking as it does the entrance of living interests into sacred painting. The bustle and movement that earlier masters had not ventured to present are seen here to the greatest advantage, and although there must have been many to declare that its conception was wicked and irreligious and quite outside the thought of such acknowledged masters as Beato Angelico and Gian Bellini, it is likely that such criticism would have very little effect upon Titian, because he went on painting altar-pieces without reverting in any instance to the methods of his predecessors.

He painted a "Madonna" for the Church of St Nicholas, an "Assumption" for Verona's Cathedral, an "Entombment of Christ," now in Paris, and it could have surprised nobody when the Doge Andrea Gritti commissioned the artist to decorate the Church of St. Nicholas in the Ducal Palace. These frescoes have disappeared, but a picture by Titian preserves the patron for us, and this is something to be grateful for, because the head is full of interest. Titian continued to paint ecclesiastical subjects until pressure from the world beyond forced him to turn his brush to other purposes, and then he came under the patronage of Frederic Gonzaga, Duke of Mantua, son of that Isabella d'Este, who had commissioned Titian's old master, Gian Bellini, to paint a secular picture for her *camerino* and was in the next few years to have her own portrait painted by Bellini's young pupil. In addition to an original picture he copied a portrait painted when she was young, and doubtless he was sufficiently a courtier to paint it in fashion that merited her approval and consoled her for having grown old.

The instinct for the fine arts had descended to Isabella's son, and when Titian went to work in Mantua he painted pictures that extended his European fame, because as the western world was situated in those days Mantua had a word to say in its affairs, entertaining foreign potentates and receiving foreign ambassadors. In those days, too, ambassadors took note of art movements, knowing that in so doing they were bound to please their masters; the political correspondence of the times includes a very considerable amount of art gossip. It is certain that Titian worked in Mantua for the Duke, and painted many pictures including the "Eleven Cæsars," but unhappily the greater part of all his labour is lost. Perhaps some canvases await the discerning critic in half-forgotten gallery or lumber-rooms; it is not likely that all have been destroyed.

The next great Italian house with which Titian seems to have entered into relations was that of Urbino whose Duke was nephew of that Pope Julius II. who was known to his contemporaries as "the Terrible Pontiff" because of his uncontrollable temper. He was the Pope who gave Michelangelo the commission to paint the ceiling in the Sistine Chapel. This artist was at least as bad-tempered as the Terrible Pontiff and the "I'm not a painter" with which he greeted the Pontiff's demand that he should paint when he preferred to practise sculpture has echoed down the ages. It is worth remembering that when the work was done, and Pope Julius came to see the result, he suggested that the scaffolding should be re-erected and the work decorated afresh with ultramarine and gold-leaf! Although Pope Julius bought the "Apollo" and the "Laocoon," Michelangelo was his adviser, but his nephew Francesco Maria della Rovere had sound instinct, and his connection with Titian lasted as long as he lived.

In the early years of this connection Titian painted the Duke and Duchess and the famous "Bella," which is reproduced in these pages and is reckoned, in spite of repainting, to be one of the most notable works from Titian's hand in this period of his career. Many portraits painted for the Court of Urbino are mentioned by Vasari; we cannot find any traces of them to-day. As one of them was of the Turkish Sultan, and it is not on record that Titian ever went to Turkey, it is reasonable to suppose that some at least of these pictures were copies of portraits that other men had painted. It was the custom for foreign potentates to have their portrait painted by the best man in their own capital and then to send the portrait to be copied by some artist of world-wide repute.

In the Uffizi Gallery in Florence there are portraits of the Duke of Urbino (which are signed) and his Duchess; they were kept at Urbino until the early part of the seventeenth century, and were then brought to their present resting-place. The picture of the Duke is a very striking one. He had made a great reputation in fighting against the Turks, and the emblems of his high office are seen in the picture. The Duchess is painted in repose; like so many of Titian's portraits of women this one has a rather listless expression. When the Duke died his son Guidobaldo continued relations with the painter, who painted the Duchess Julia just before her death. It seems likely that she never saw the picture, which is now in the Pitti at Florence. The portrait of the husband is lost.

II

MIDDLE AGE

This brief and rather hurried review of Titian's life and work has brought us to his middle age and we find him now almost at the zenith of his fame, though his powers have not yet reached their ripest and fullest expression. Venice, Mantua, and Urbino have acknowledged his talent, while if Pope and Sultan have not actually sat to him for their portraits they have sent him other men's work to copy. The great Charles V., who seemed bent upon holding all western and central Europe in the hollow of his hand, was his friend and patron, and we see what manner of man he was from the pictures in the Prado. The first, painted in the very early years of their acquaintance, shows Charles with a great hound by his side. His right hand rests on his dagger, his left on the dog's collar, he wears the chain of the Golden Fleece, and seems a man born to command. Belonging, of course, to a much later date is the other portrait of Charles at the Battle of Mühlburg, perhaps even less a monument of Titian's skill than an enduring record of the terrible craze for repainting that beset Spain until recent years, and is not unknown to-day, though public opinion has had some effect even in Madrid. It is not generally known that there is a Spanish official who has a salaried engagement to assist the old masters whose work shows signs of fading, and without wishing to be hypercritical it is reasonable to remark that these officials in a laudable anxiety to earn their stipend have done irreparable damage to much work that they were not fit to approach.

In spite of the imminence of the political scheme that occupied the mind of Charles V. he was able to spare time to consider the affairs of art, and his attitude towards Titian seems to have been that of one friend towards another rather than that of an emperor towards a foreign painter. It is interesting in this connection to remember that his son Philip II., who succeeded to the throne of Spain, was a patron of the arts, that Philip III. was not indifferent to them, that Philip IV. was the friend as well as the patron of Velazquez, and that Velazquez admired Titian above all the other Venetians, and is said to have copied many of his pictures.

Charles proceeded to put the crown upon Titian's reputation by sending him in 1533 a patent of nobility, and making him a Knight of the Order of the Golden Spur. Among the stories that receive a sort of sanction from age is one to the effect that Charles V. once picked up a brush that Titian had dropped, and said to his astonished courtiers that such a man was worthy of having an emperor to serve him. Stories of this kind seem to flourish in Spain. Students of the life of Velazquez will not forget the legend that Philip IV. painted the cross of St. Iago upon the painter's cloak when he saw the famous picture "Las Meniñas," in order to give the most fitting expression of his admiration. This story contrasts strangely with the true facts of the case. Charles went even further than to give the patent of nobility to Titian, he made a determined effort to persuade him to live in Madrid altogether. Very wisely Titian refused the offers; he was a Venetian at heart, and a free man. To be a citizen of Venice was an honour for which even a Charles V. could hardly find an effective substitute.

There is no reason to believe that Titian would have fared any better in the wind-swept, heat-stricken capital of Spain than Velazquez fared in the years that brought Philip IV. to the throne.

At the splendid court of Charles V. Titian would soon have become a mere official painter, he would have been compelled to paint to order and endure the snubs and buffets of the blue-blooded, but uncultivated courtiers attached to the royal establishment. Moreover, the Venetians did not like Spanish methods of dealing with matters of art and faith; to Titian their attitude would have appeared intolerable.

Although he was a painter, Titian had little of the temperament that is generally associated with artists. His genius was allied to sound commercial instincts, and he chose for intimates and advisers men whose practical experience of the world and of affairs was at least as great as his own, in some cases even greater. Of these Pietro Aretino, father of modern journalists, was one of the most sagacious and quite the most remarkable. His voluminous letters tell us a great deal about Titian to whom he played the part of mentor, and they reveal the writer as a man of great shrewdness who moved in the highest circles in many cities, living largely by his wits, and wielding a pen that was often sharper than a sword and was certainly more feared. He found Titian as valuable to him as he was useful to Titian, and, when any delicate negotiations were to the fore Aretino's large circle of friends and patrons, his ready tongue and fluent pen were at the service of the painter. His portrait painted by Titian was till recently in Rome and reveals a man with massive head, sagacious expression, and a curious likeness to Dr. Hans Richter the famous musician. His letters are still read with interest by those who like to look back over the course of life in the sixteenth century.

At a time when he had passed middle age, Titian would seem to have exhausted for the moment the possibilities of Venice. We have seen that the Fathers of the City had been a little vexed with his delay in painting the "Battle of Cadore" in the Hall of the Grand Council. He had received a State allowance in order to enable him to paint it, and twenty years had not sufficed him for the completion of the commission. When he was threatened with the loss of his money and dignities by the indignant Councillors, whose patience at the end of two decades was quite stale, he did set to work, and satisfied them that the picture was worth the waiting. But they could hardly have been inclined to extend much more patronage to a man who allowed the rulers of other States to turn his attention from commissioned work, and never hesitated to leave it for years at a time when other and more remunerative orders came to hand. Moreover the great churches were fairly well filled, and the smaller ones could hardly afford to employ the greatest master of the day. So Pietro Aretino, perhaps casting about to do his friend a good turn, bethought him of his influence in Rome, and addressed certain letters to the leading lights of Mother Church who were to be found there. These letters were doubtless supervised by Titian himself, because they bear a striking likeness in phraseology to the petition the painter had addressed to the Council of Ten in the days when he was little known, and Gian Bellini was still working for the State. Then, it will be remembered, the painter declared that he had been asked to go to Rome but preferred to stay in Venice; now Aretino told the Romans that Titian had been invited to go to Madrid but preferred to work in Rome. So it happened early in the 'forties that, through the useful Aretino, Titian entered into relations with the Farnese family, who were represented in the Papal Chair by Pope Paul III. The result was that Titian was invited to Ferrara, where he met the Pope and painted his portrait.

The whole correspondence, so far as it can be seen, would seem to suggest that Titian and Aretino managed this business exceedingly well. When the painter found that his ambition was within measurable distance of being gratified, and that his graceless elder son for whom he had entered a special plea, was to receive a benefice, he seems to have remembered that Venice held many attractions for him, and that he could not leave it in a hurry. Not until the close of 1545 did he visit the Eternal City, only to regret that the greater part of his life had been passed outside its walls.

As soon as he was established in Rome, Titian found himself

received by princes and prelates in fashion befitting his age and reputation. And Giorgio Vasari, the author of the great work on Italian artists, was commissioned, by one of the heads of the house of Farnese, to show the painter the wonders of the city.

To the Farnese family Titian's visit was of the first importance because its Pope and Cardinal were his first patrons, and he painted many pictures for them. Paul III. was no more than ten years older than the painter and had not long to live. He sat to Titian several times; two of the portraits are to be seen in Naples and there are others to be seen elsewhere. In addition to the fine memorials of the Farnese Pope, Naples holds several of Titian's masterpieces, including the splendid "Danäe," a "Philip II.," and a "Mary Magdalen." Those who are fortunate enough to obtain access to the really remarkable collection of pictures at Naples will not forget readily the striking portraits of the old Pope.

Titian stayed less than a year in the Eternal City in spite of the preparations he had made before undertaking the journey, and then returned to Venice with many honours, but without the long desired post for his son. Perhaps his departure gave offence to people in high places, perhaps his stay there had not been altogether as satisfactory as he had expected it to be, for despite flattering offers, despite the honour of Roman citizenship conferred upon him before he went home, he refused to return. He might have gone in the end in consideration of the preferment granted to Pomponio Vecelli his scapegrace son, but Charles V. sent for him, and he went instead to Augsburg, where the Emperor who had seen the fulfilment of so many of his hopes was living in great state, surrounded by as brilliant a court as the sixteenth century knew. In Augsburg Titian painted his most famous portrait of Charles V., the one showing the Emperor on horseback, which as has been stated, is to be seen to-day in the Prado in Madrid.

Titian remained in Augsburg for the greater part of a year before he returned to Venice, to find his studio, or work-shop as it would have been called in those days besieged by the envoys of the various European rulers who were all clamouring for portraits. From Venice the painter went to Milan at the invitation of Prince Philip of Spain (afterwards Philip II.) and at the close of 1550 he was back in Augsburg where he painted several portraits of Prince Philip of which perhaps the best is in the Prado. By the time he returned to Venice he would have been in the immediate neighbourhood of his eightieth year. His brush was never idle, and if the fruit of his labours could have been preserved in fire-proof galleries the gain to the world would have been enormous. Unfortunately we have to face the unpleasant truth that considerably more than half his life work has been lost.

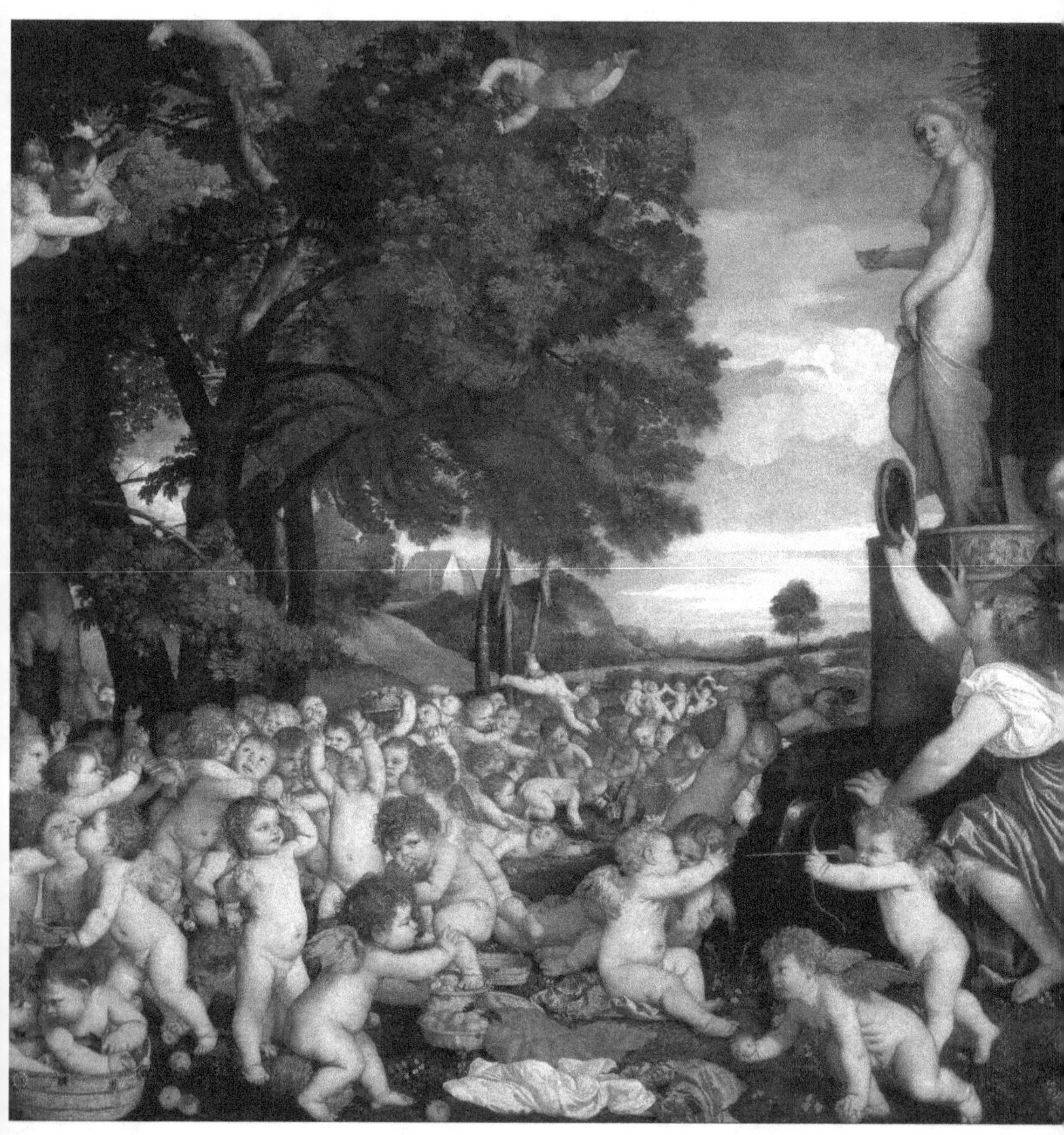

Titian, The Worship of Venus, 1518, Madrid

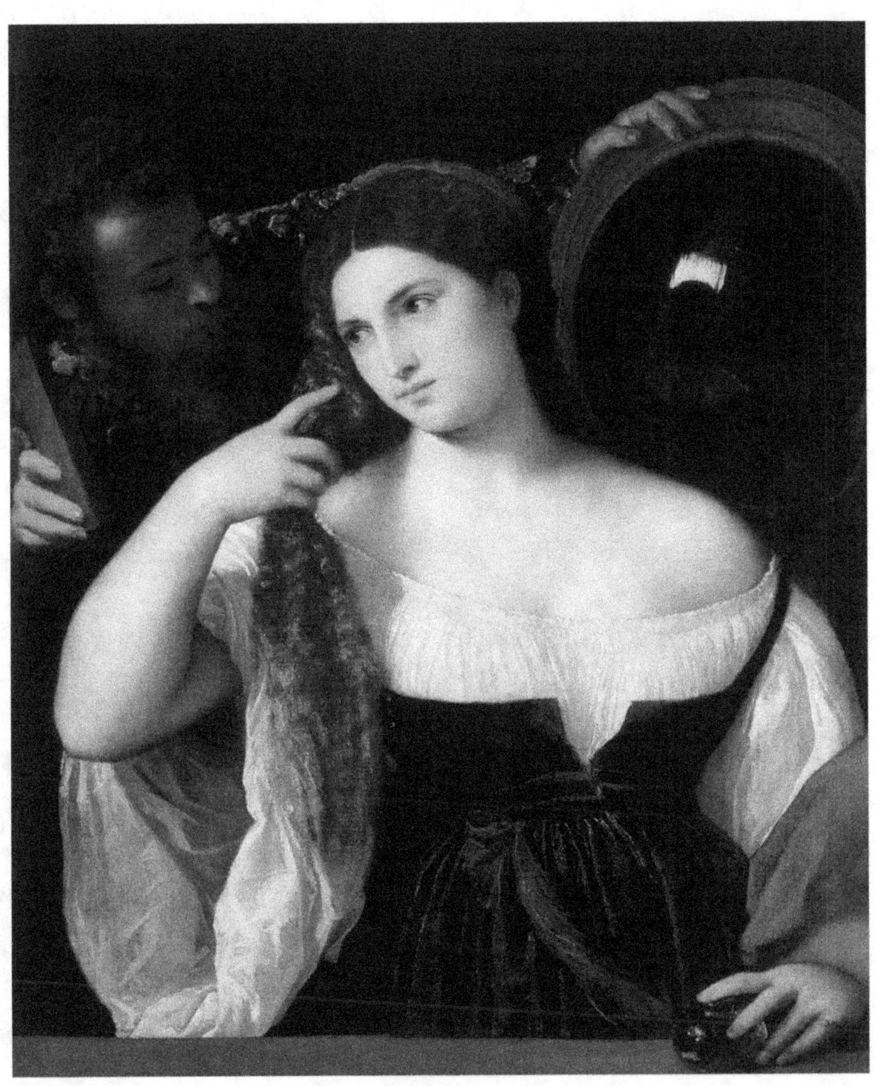

Titian, Woman With a Mirror, 1514, Louvre

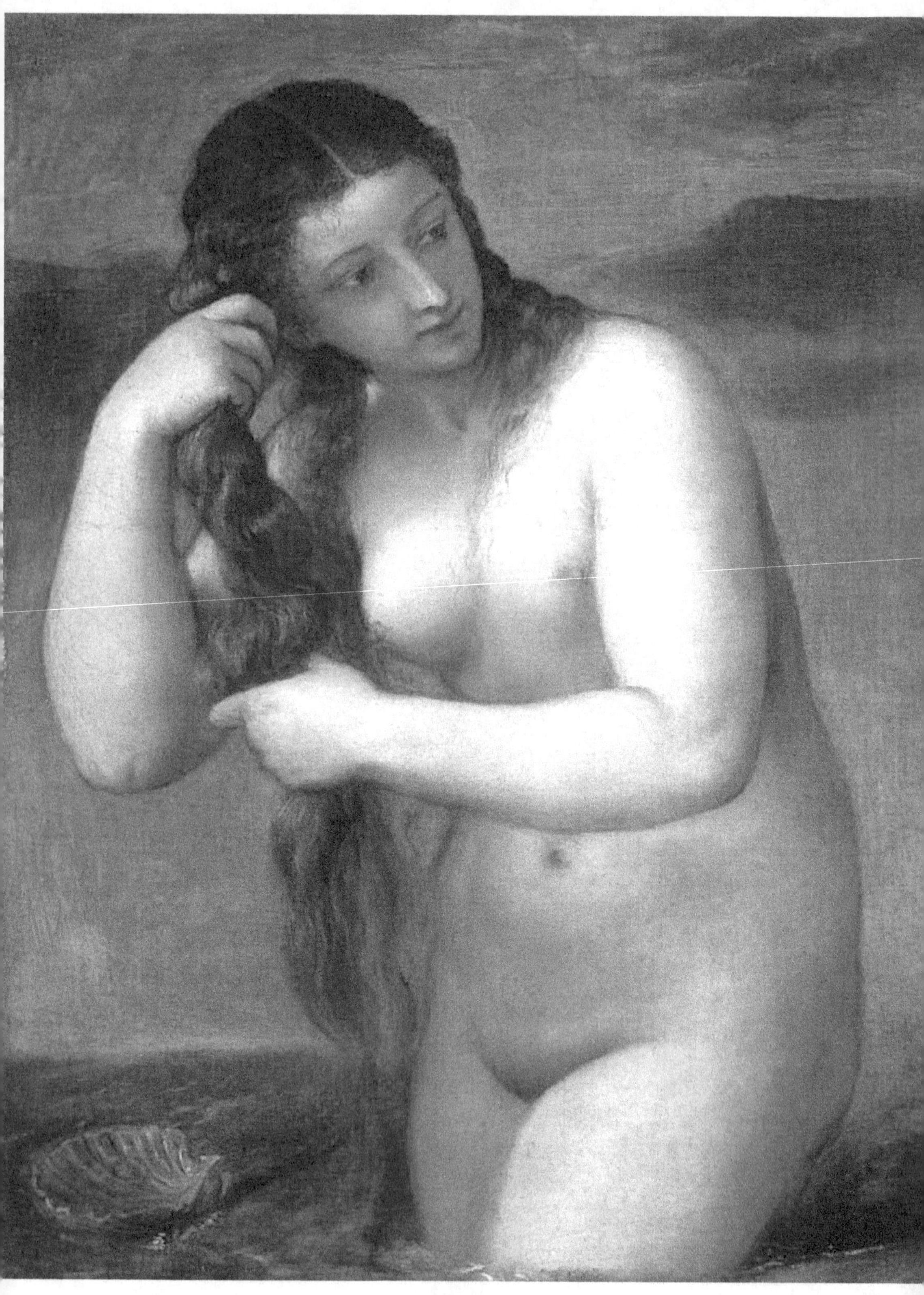

Titian, Venus Rising From the Sea, 1520, Scotland

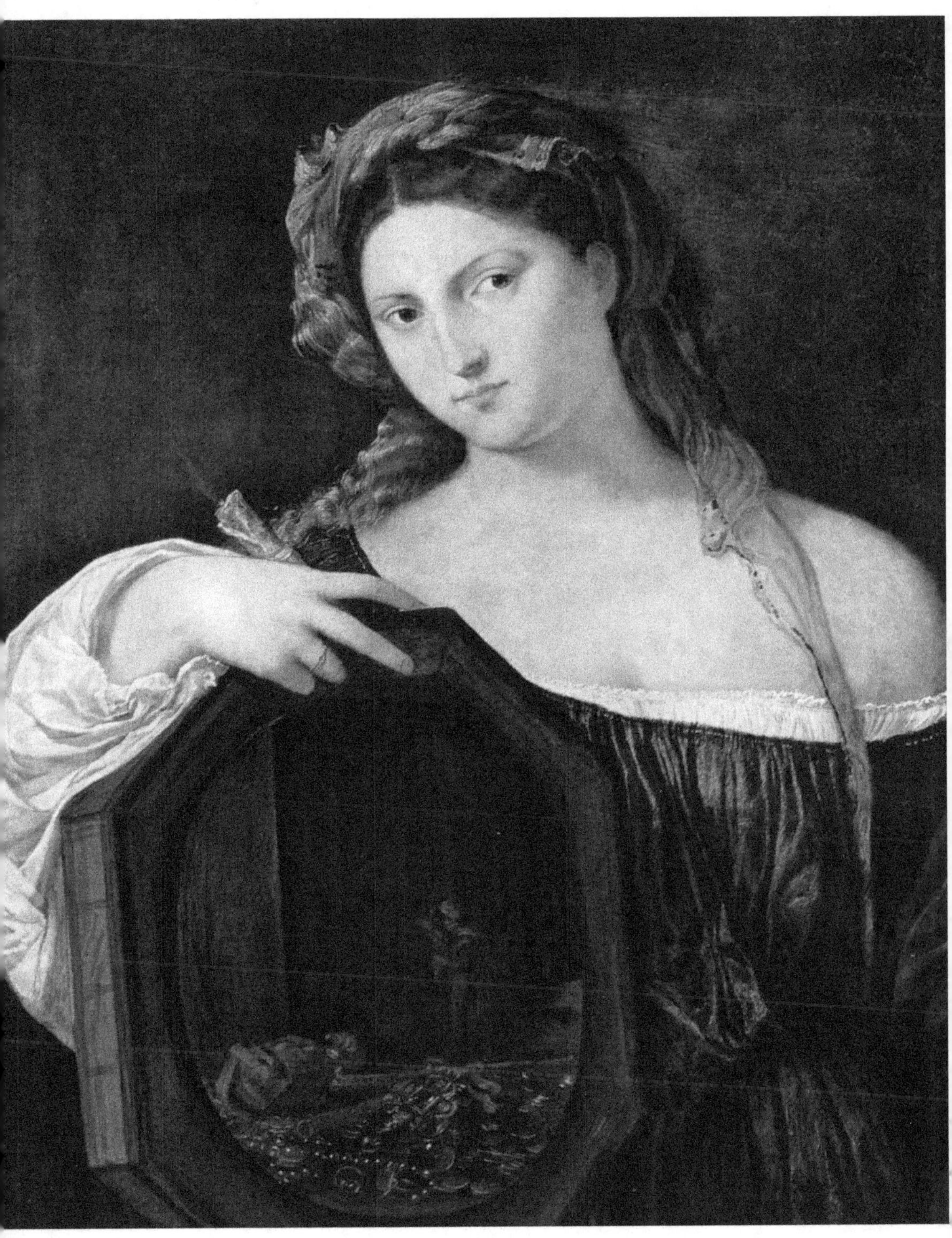

Titian, Vanita, 1511, Alte Pinakothek, München

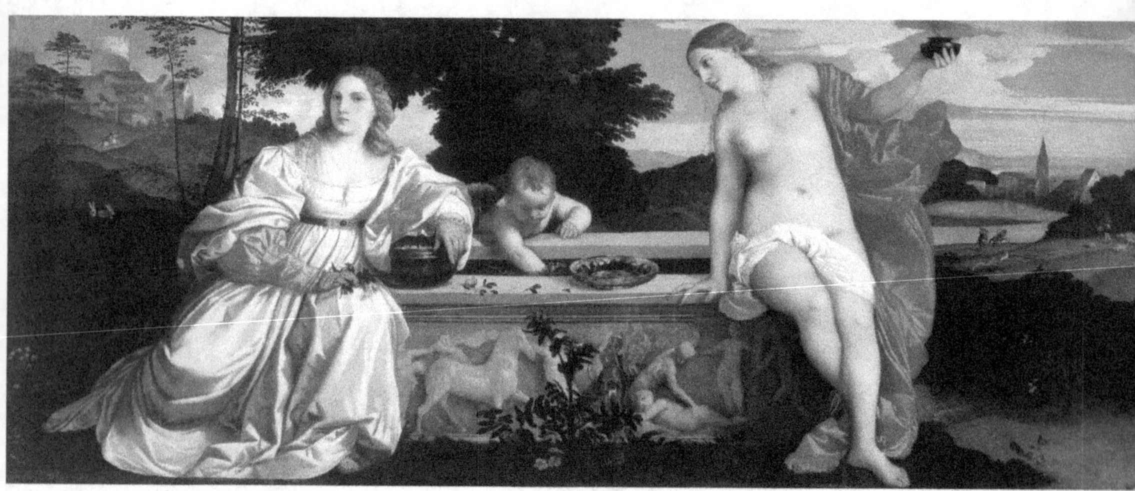

Titian, Sacred and Profane Love, 1514, Villa Borghese

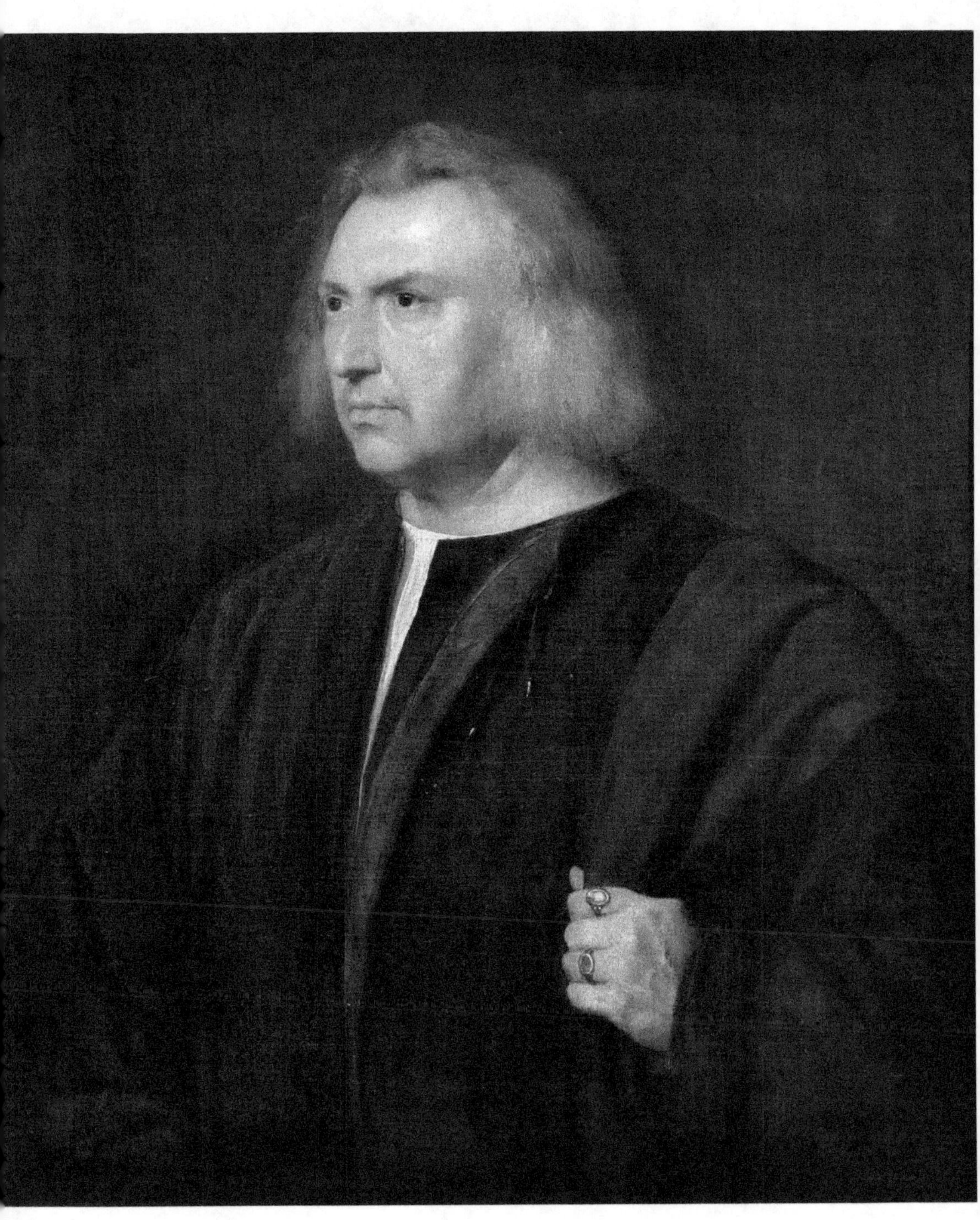

Titian, Gian Giacomo Bartolotti da Parma, 1518, Vienna

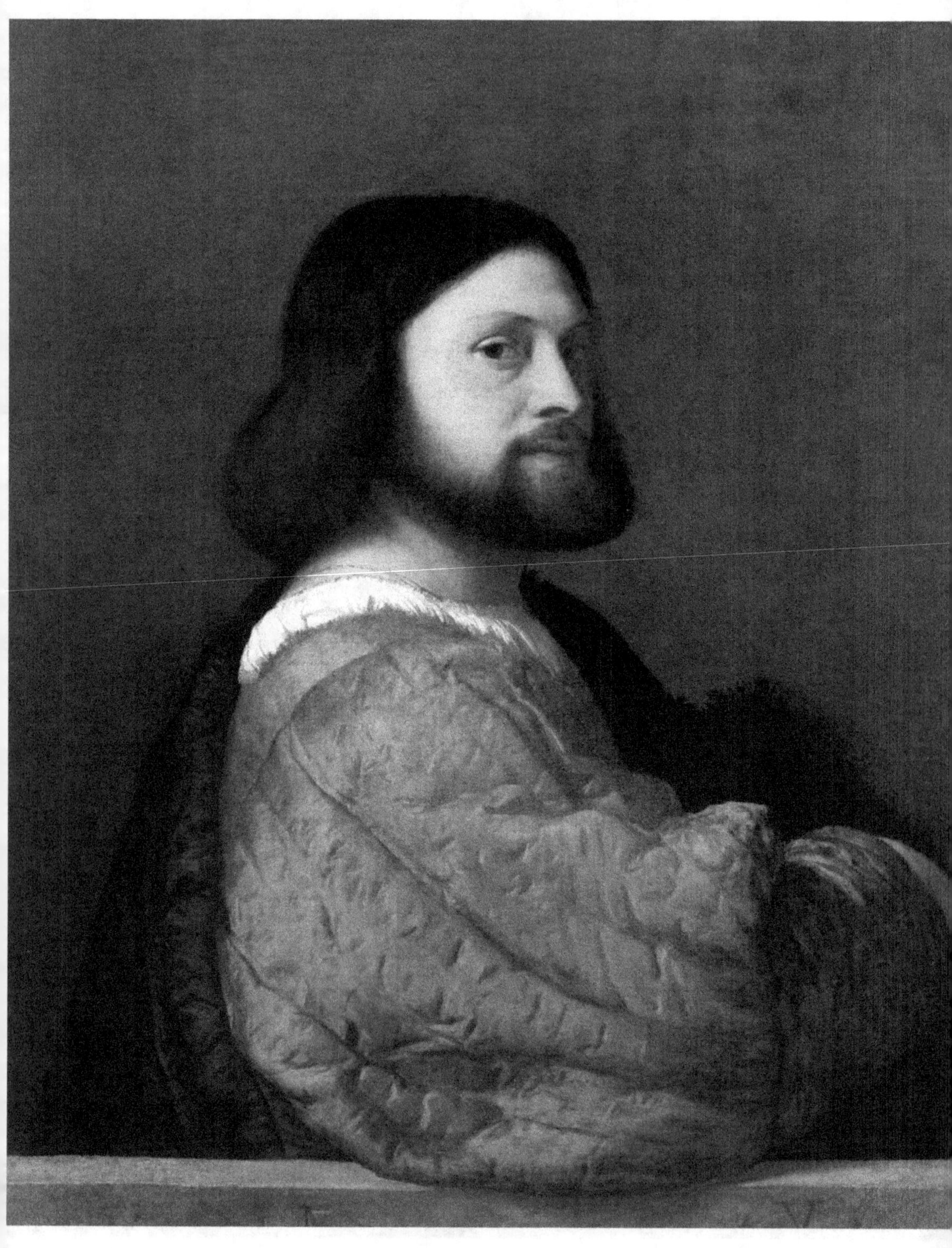

Titian, Man With the Blue Sleeve, 1510-11,
National Gallery, London

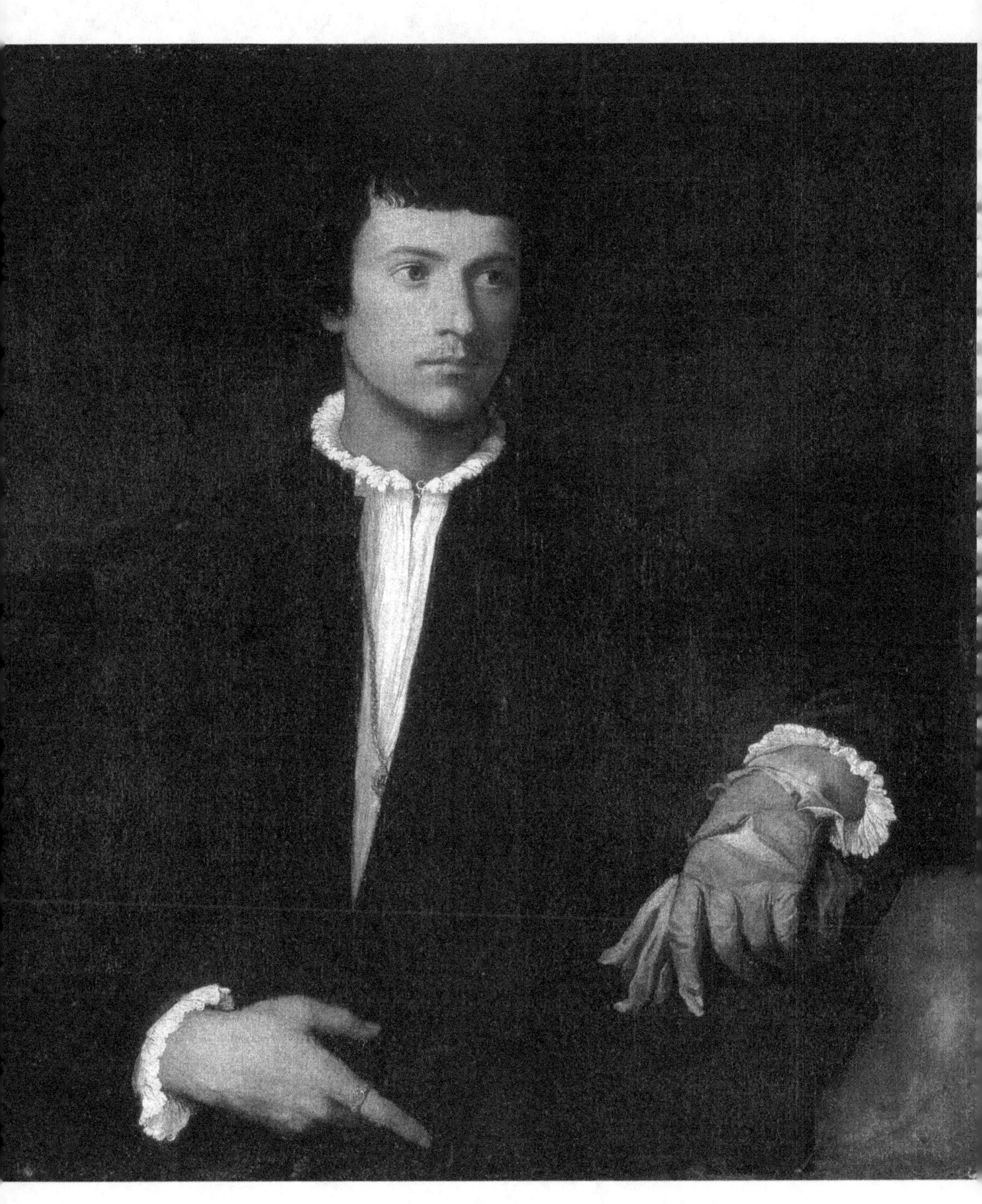

Titian, Man With a Glove, 1520, Louvre

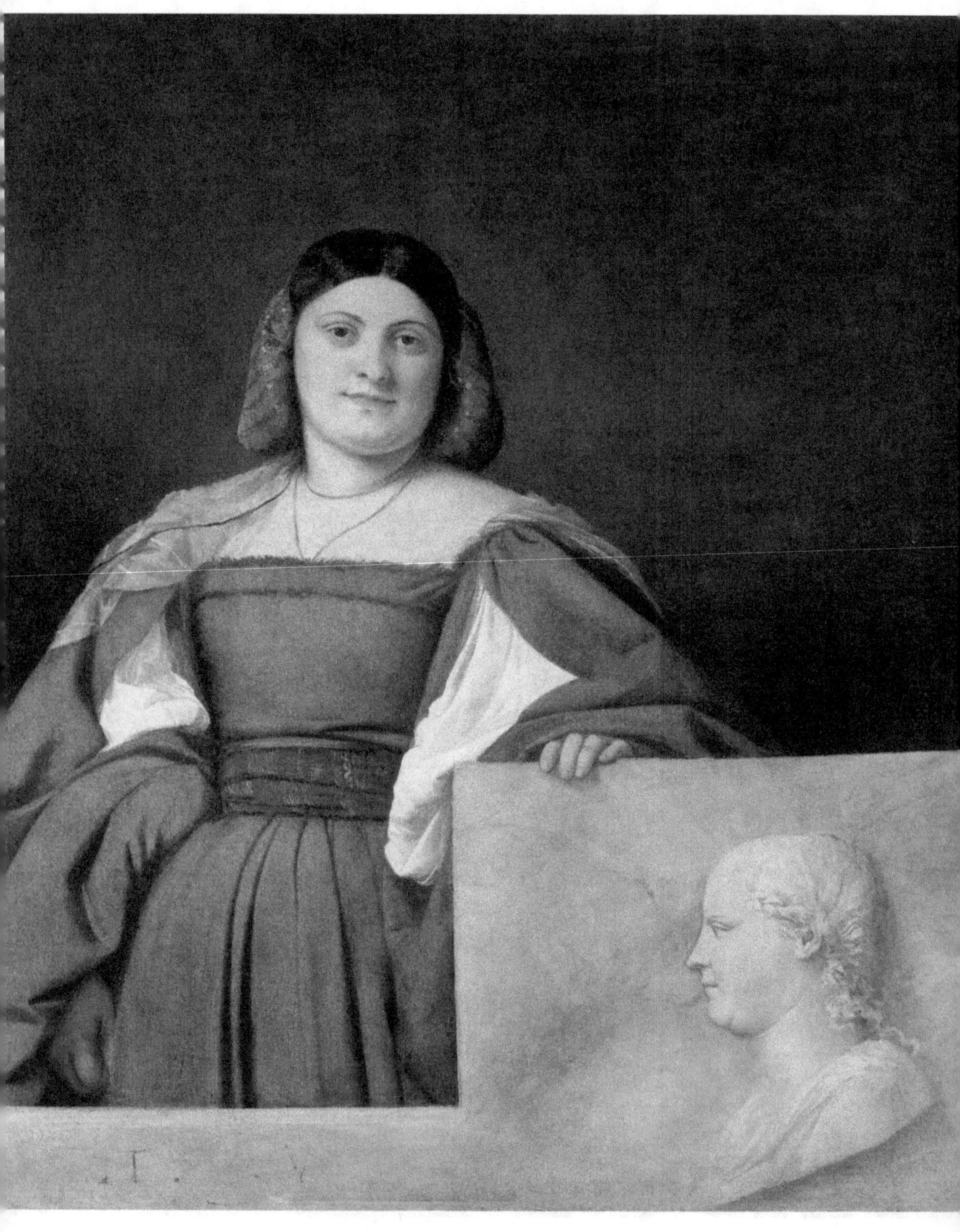

Titian, La Schiavona, 1510,
National Gallery, London

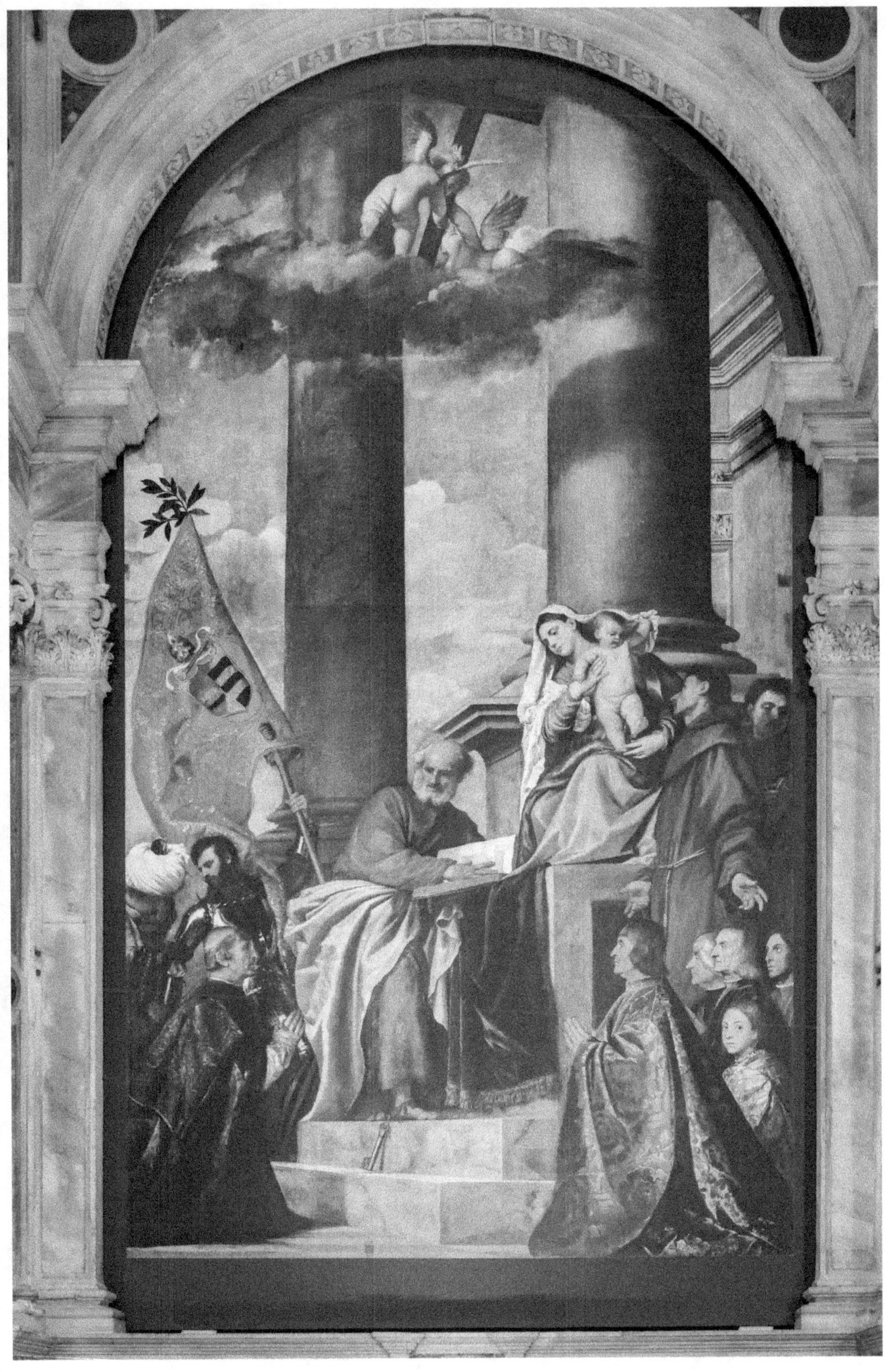

Titian, Pesaro Altarpiece, 1519-26, Friari , Venice

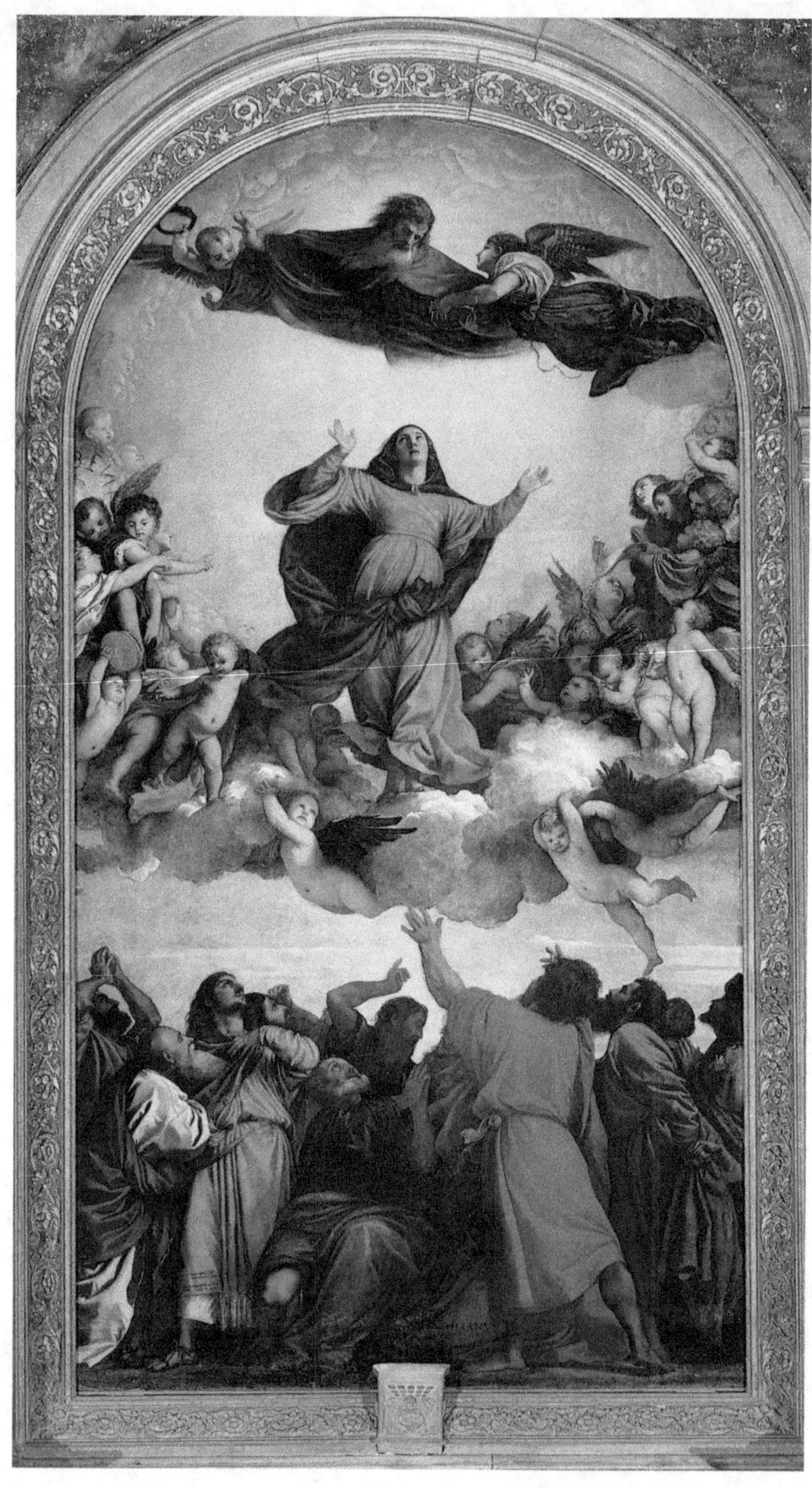

Titian, Assumption of the Virgin, 1517-18, Venice

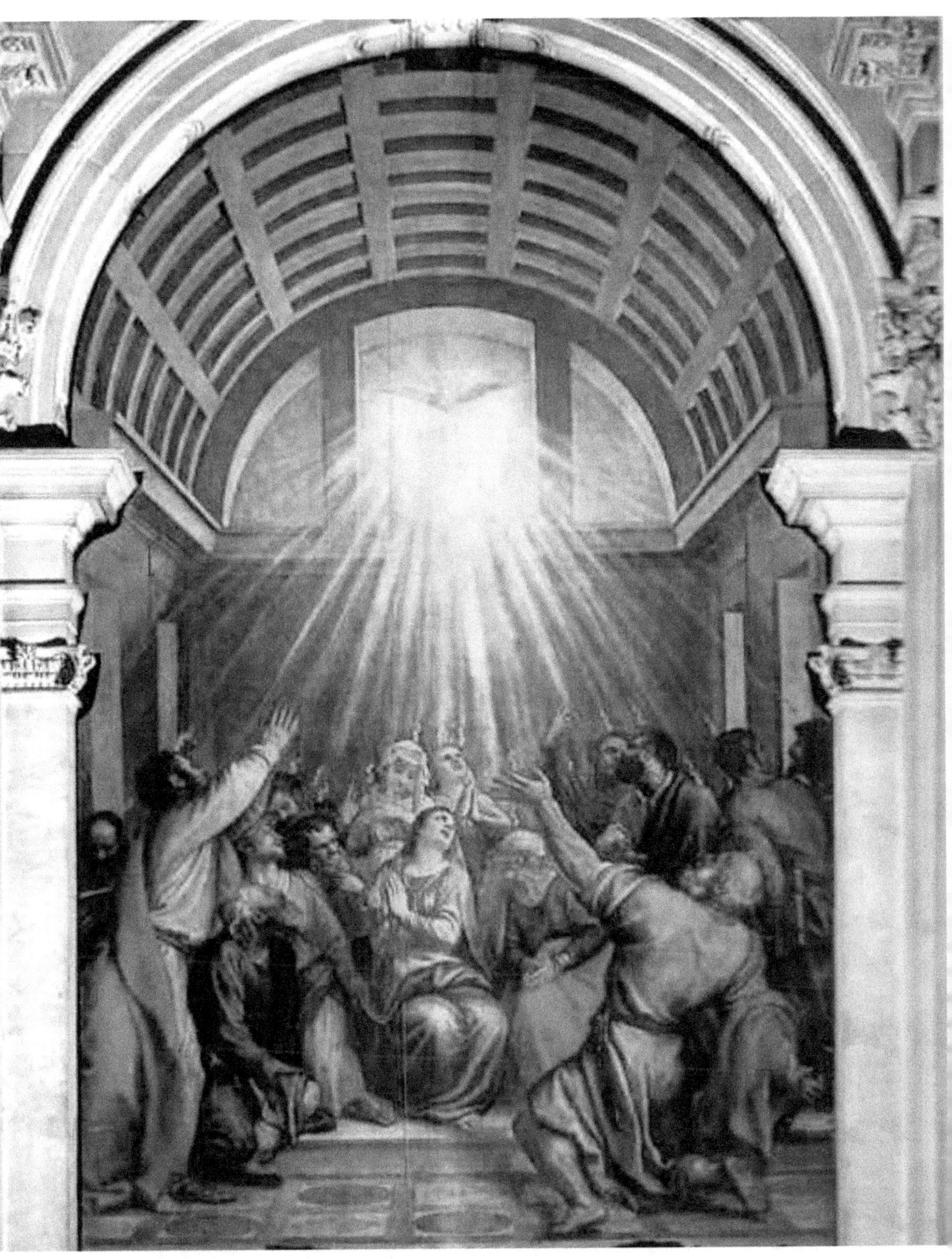

Titian, The Descent of the Holy Spirit, Venice

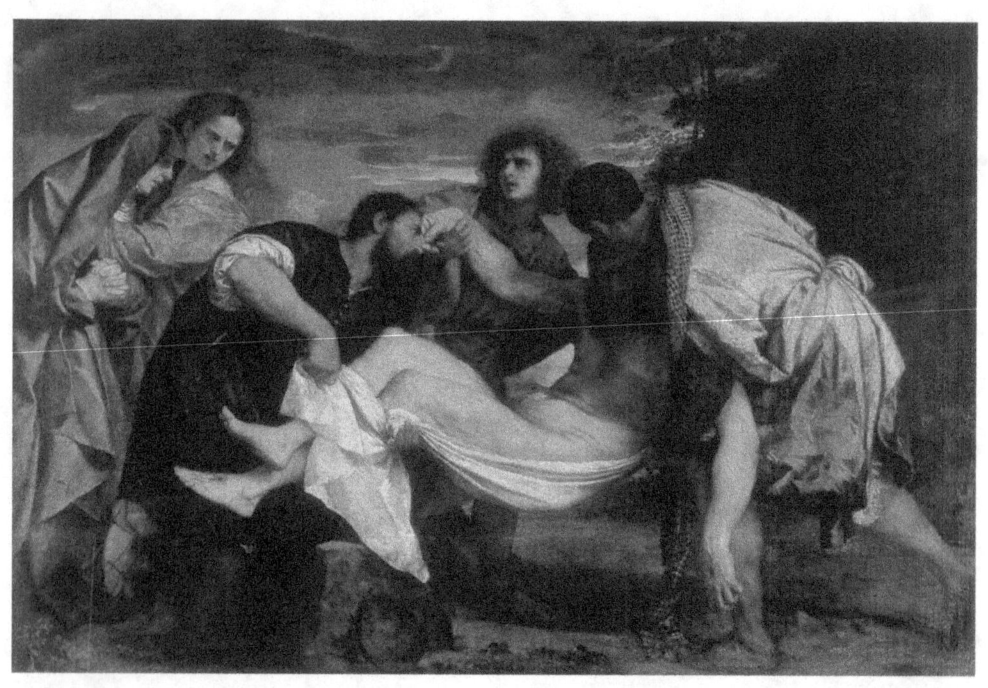

Titian, The Entombment, 1523-26, Louvre

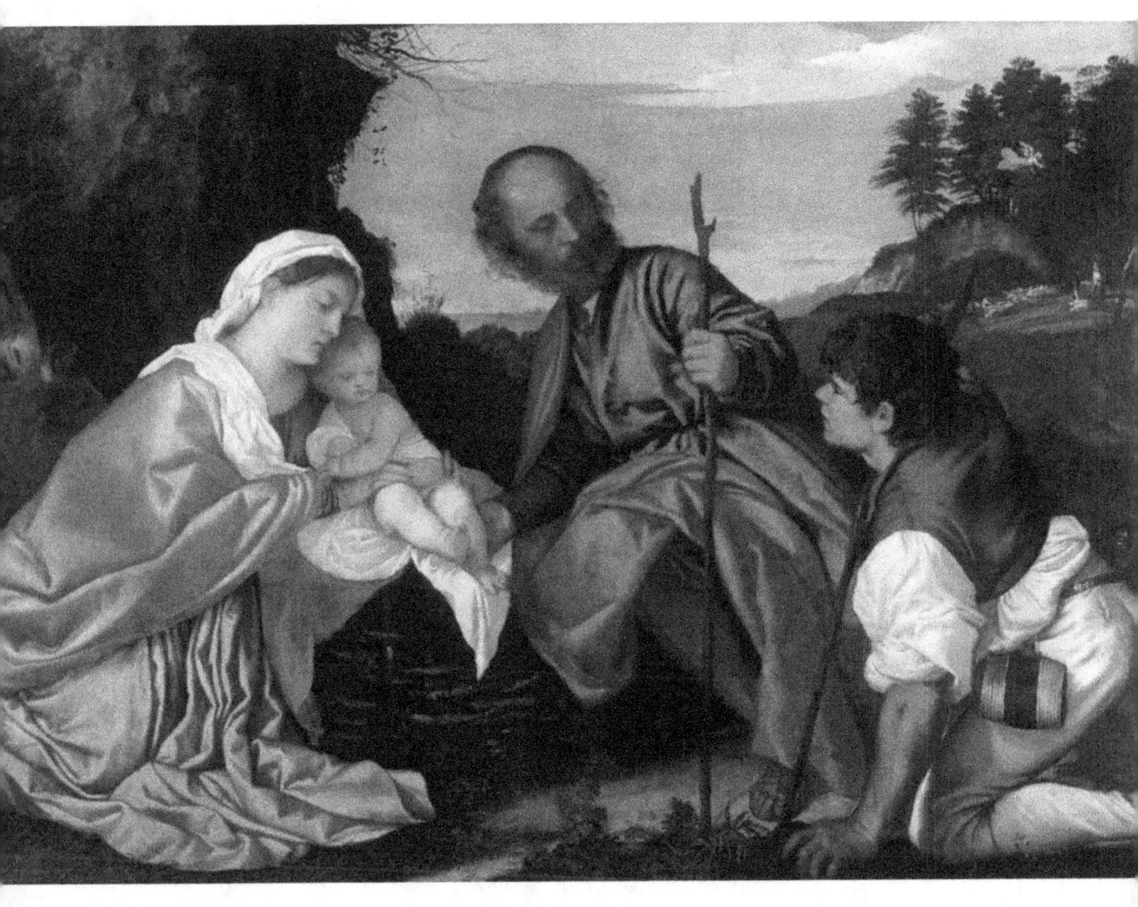

Titian, The Holy Family With a Shepherd, 1510,
National Gallery, Lndon

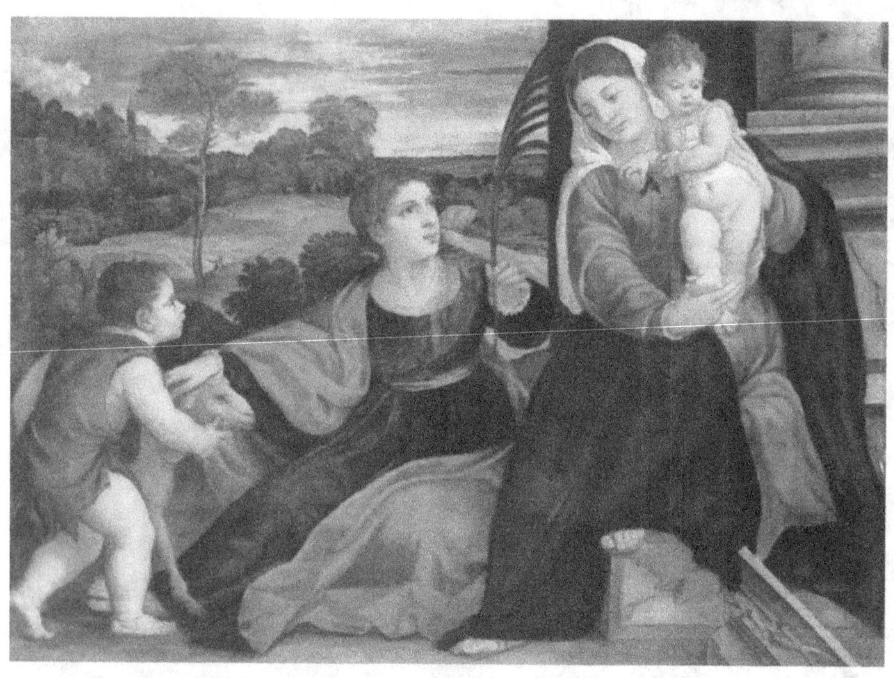

Titian, Madonna and Child With Saints Agnes and the Baptist, Dijon

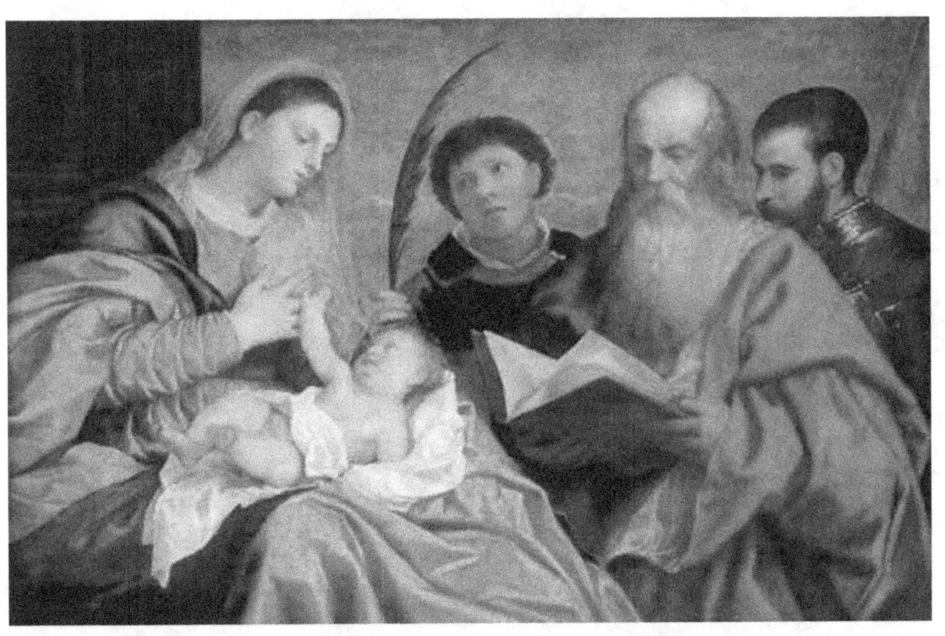

Titian, Madonna and Child With Saints, 1520, Vienna

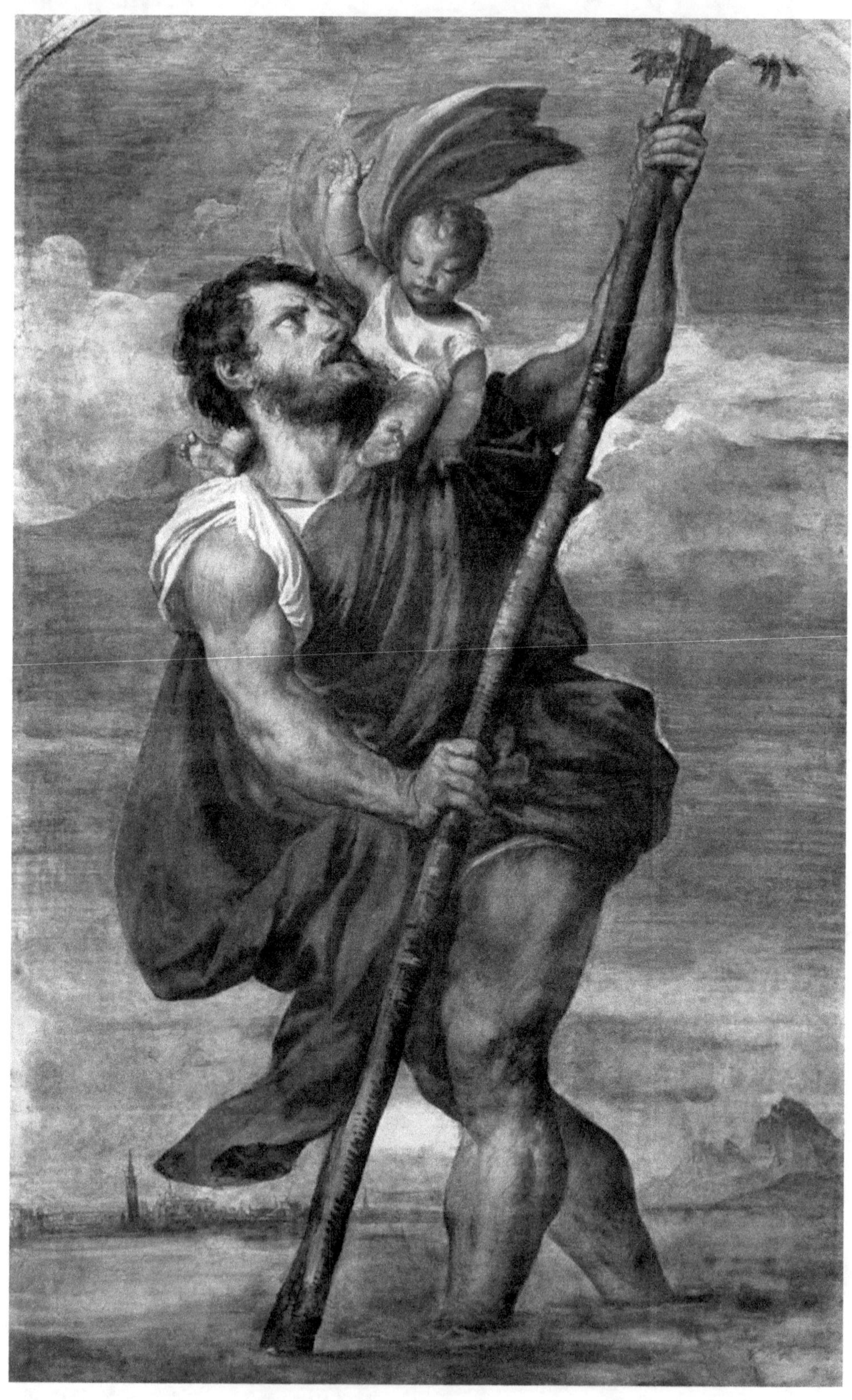

Titian, St Christopher, 1524, Venice

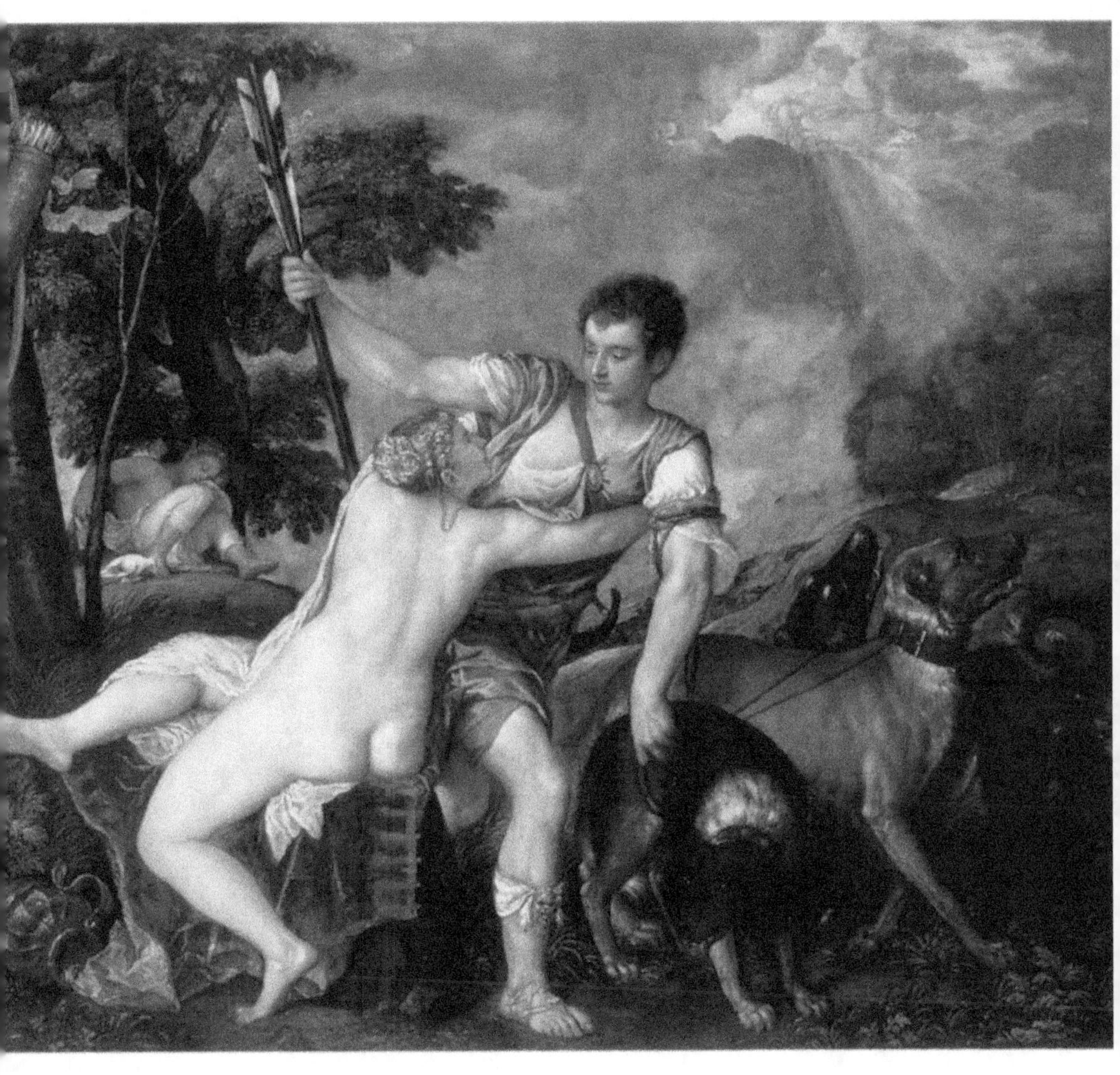

Titian, Venus and Adonis, 1550, Ashmolean, Oxford

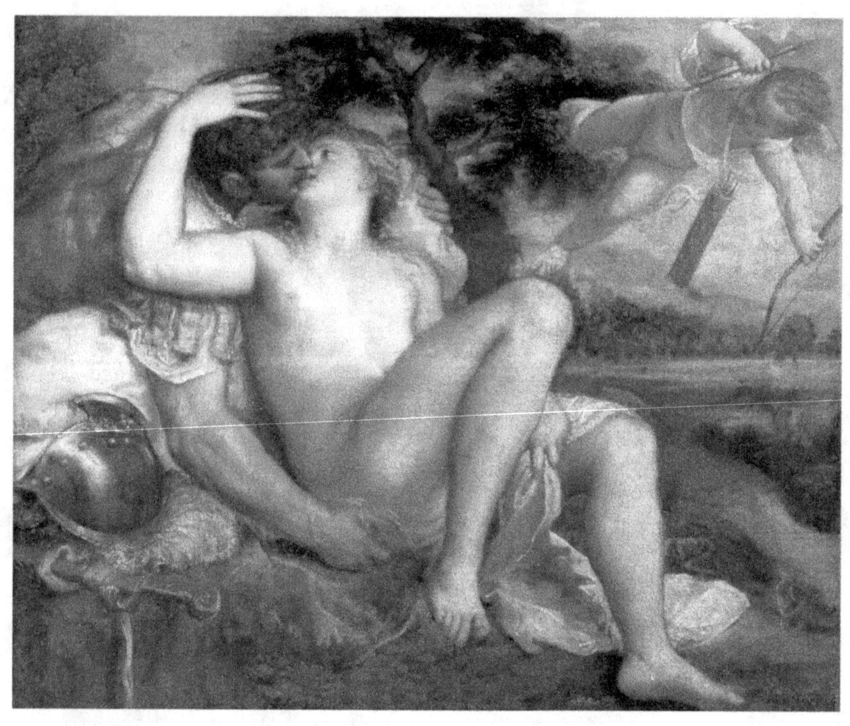

Titian, Venus and Mars and Amor, 1530, Vienna

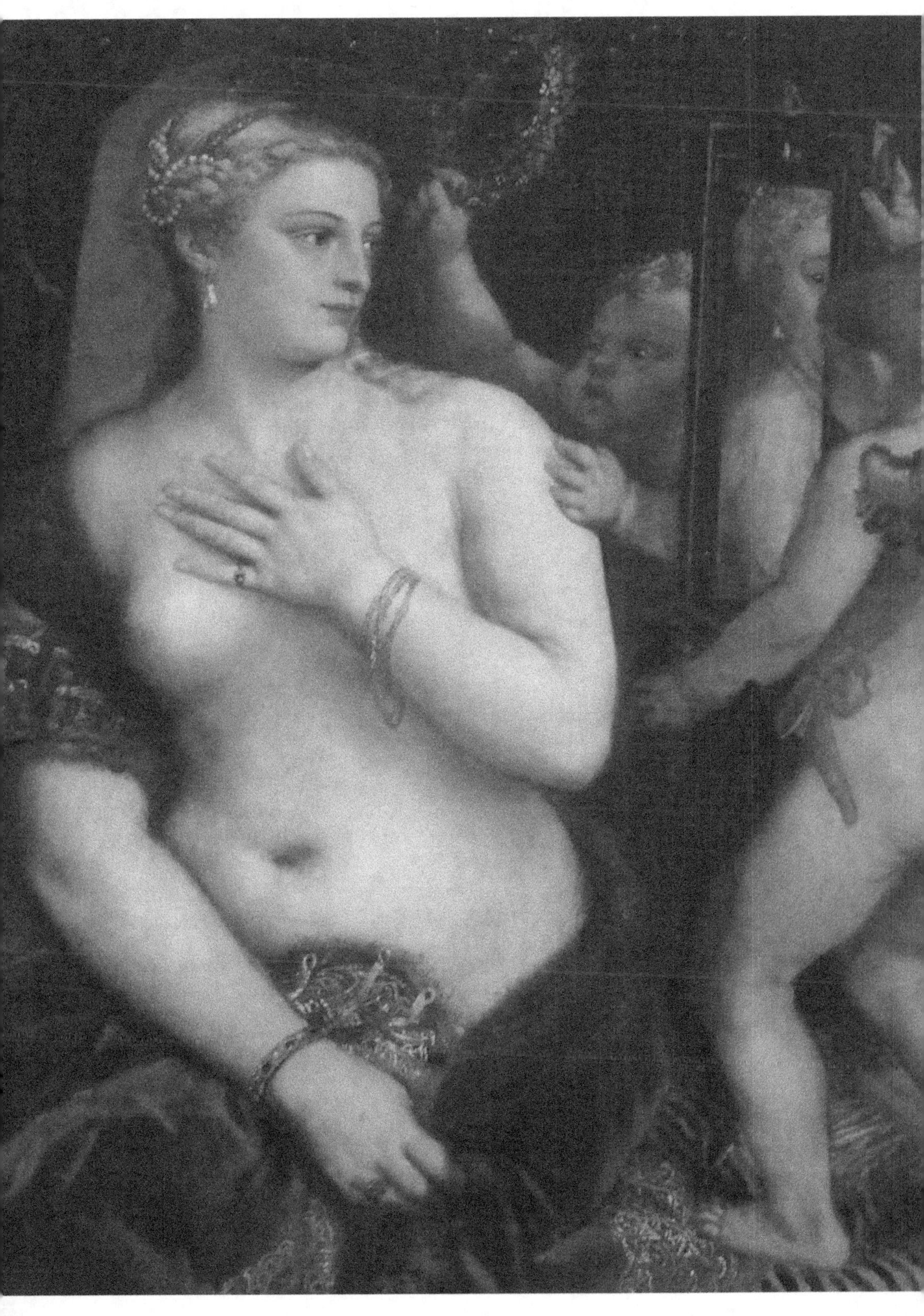

Titian, Venus With a Mirror, 1554-55, Washington, DC

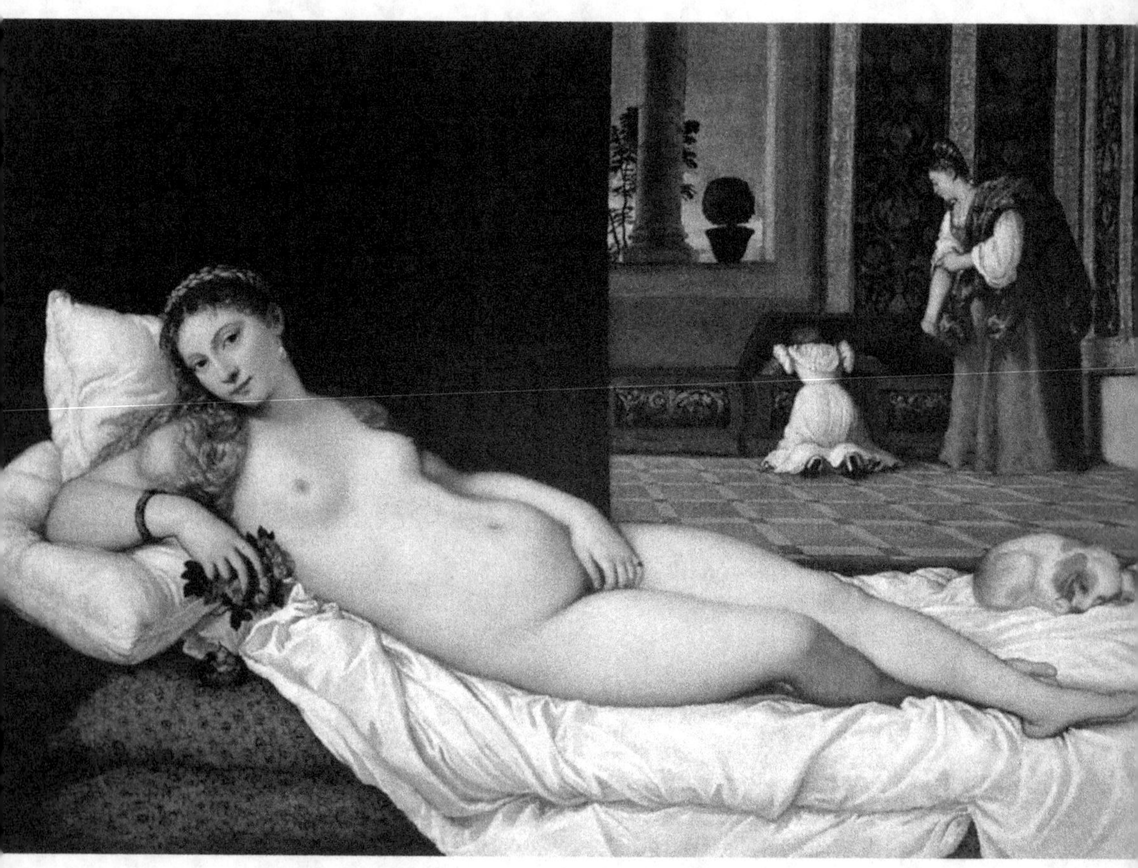

Titian, The Venus of Urbino, 1538, Uffizi, Florence

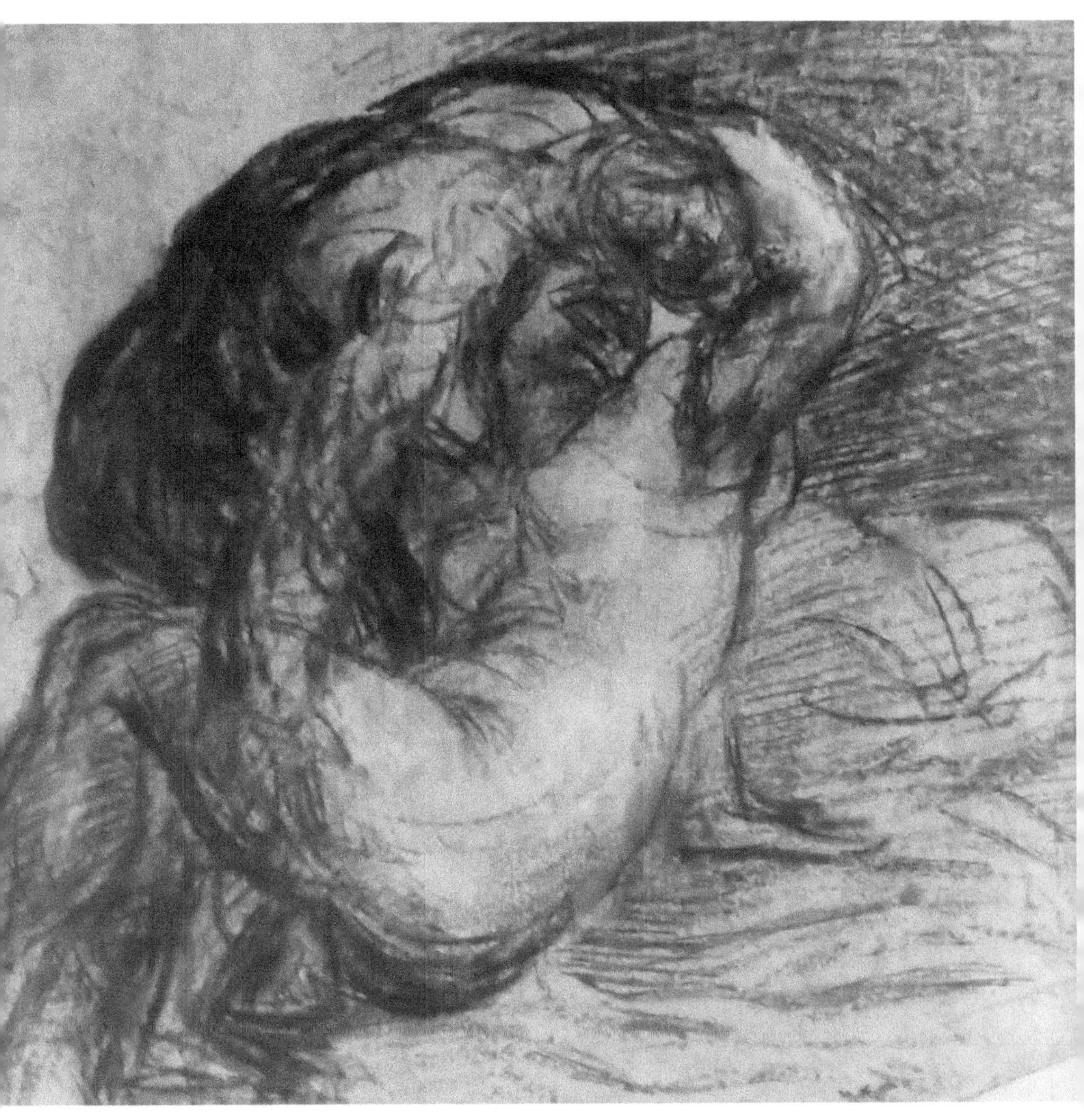

Titian, A Couple, c. 1570, Cambridge

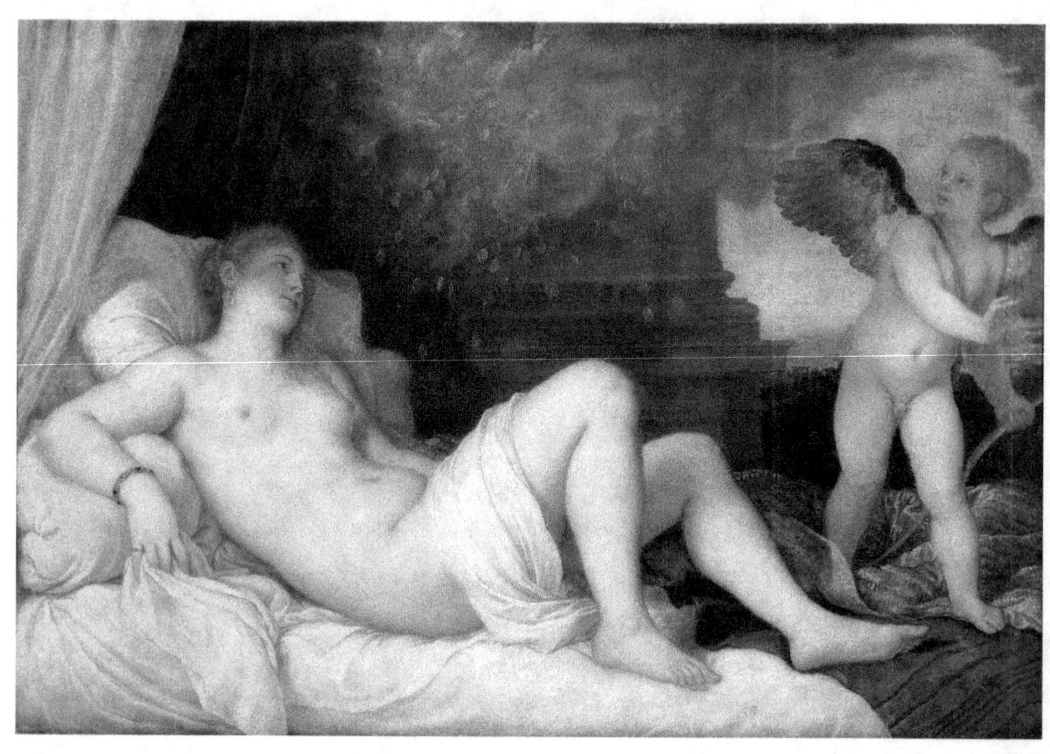

Titian, Danaë, 1544, Naples

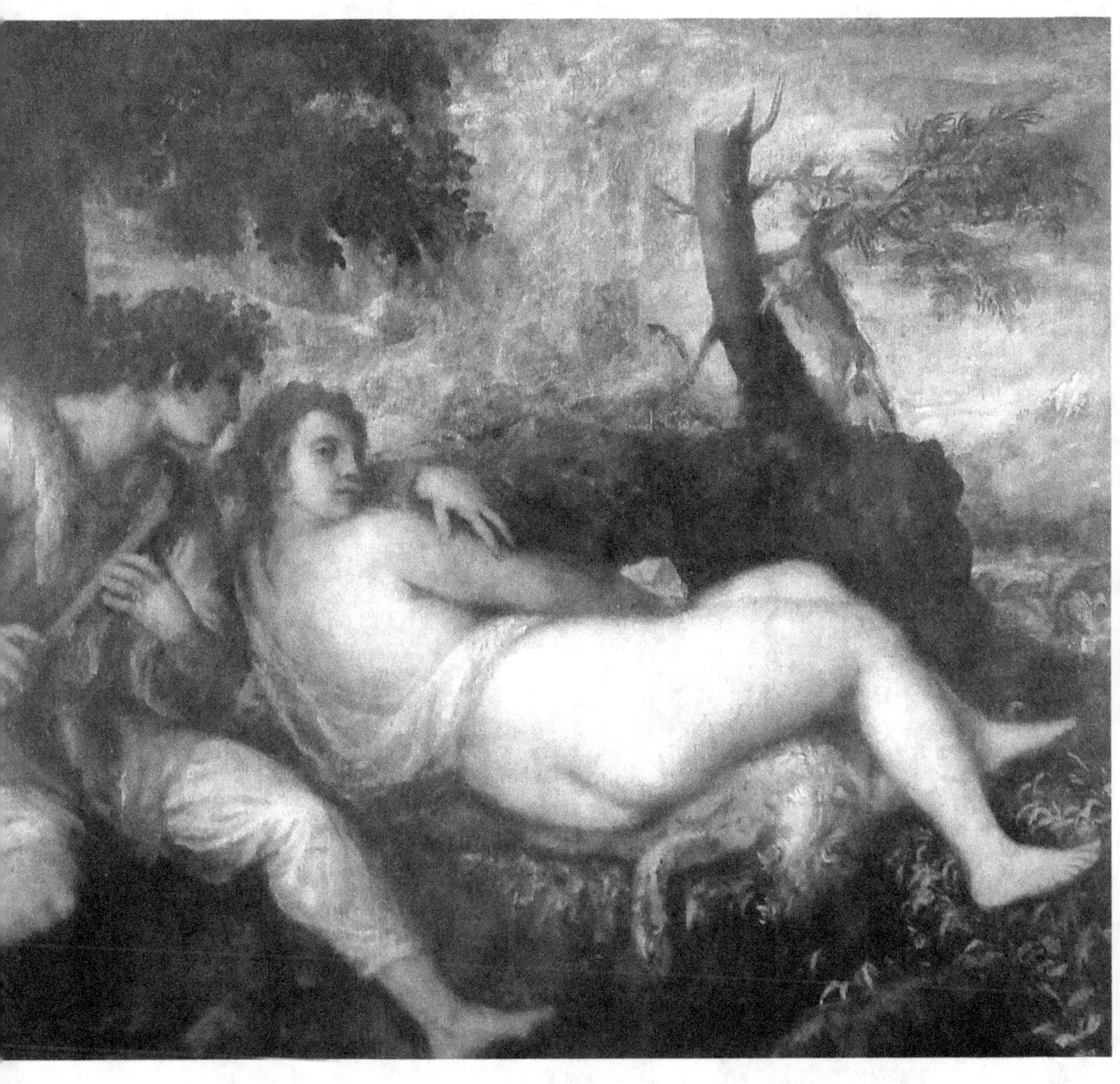

Titian, Nymph and Shepherd, 1575, Vienna

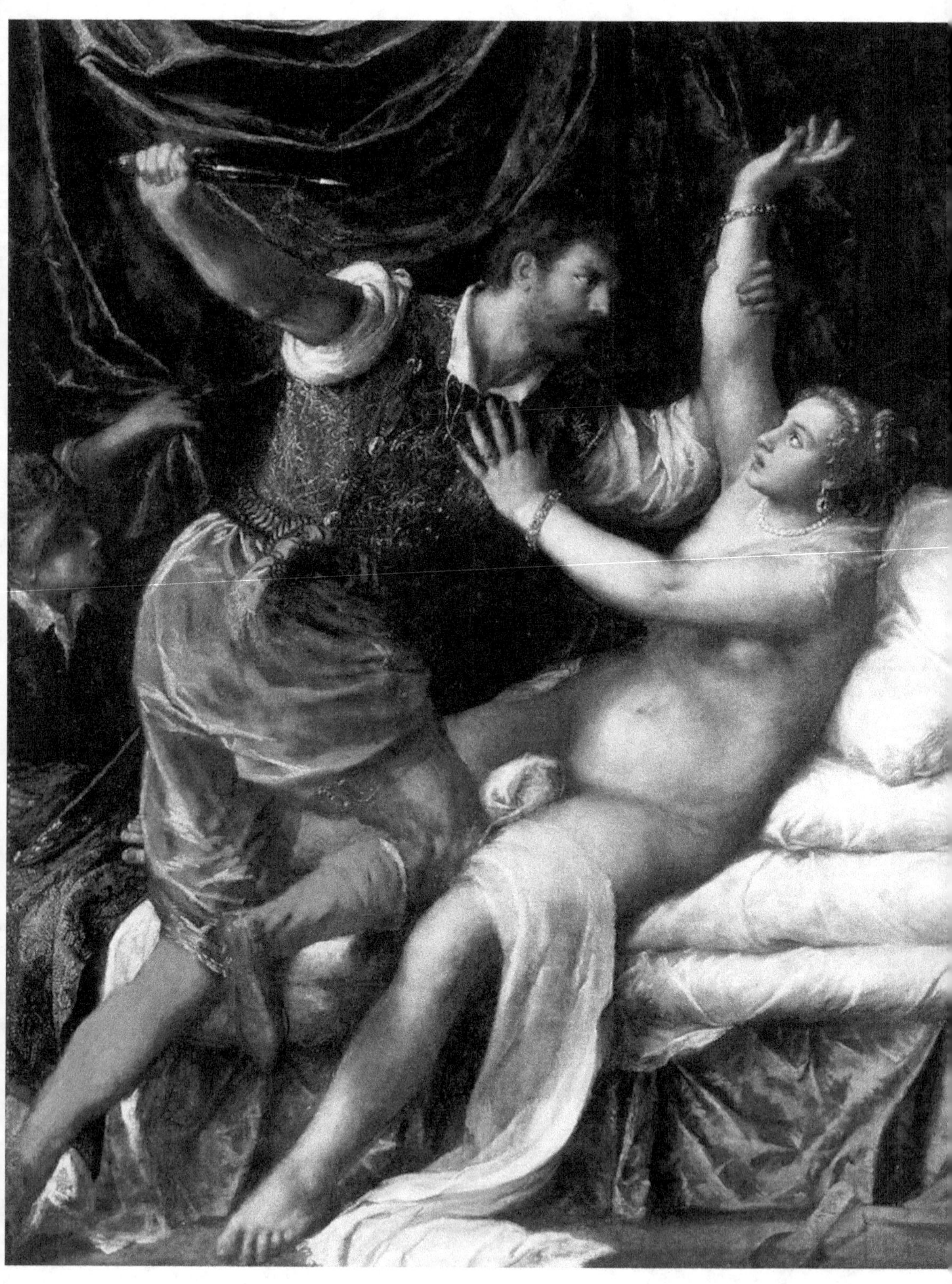

Titian, Tarquin and Lucretia, 1568-71, Cambridge

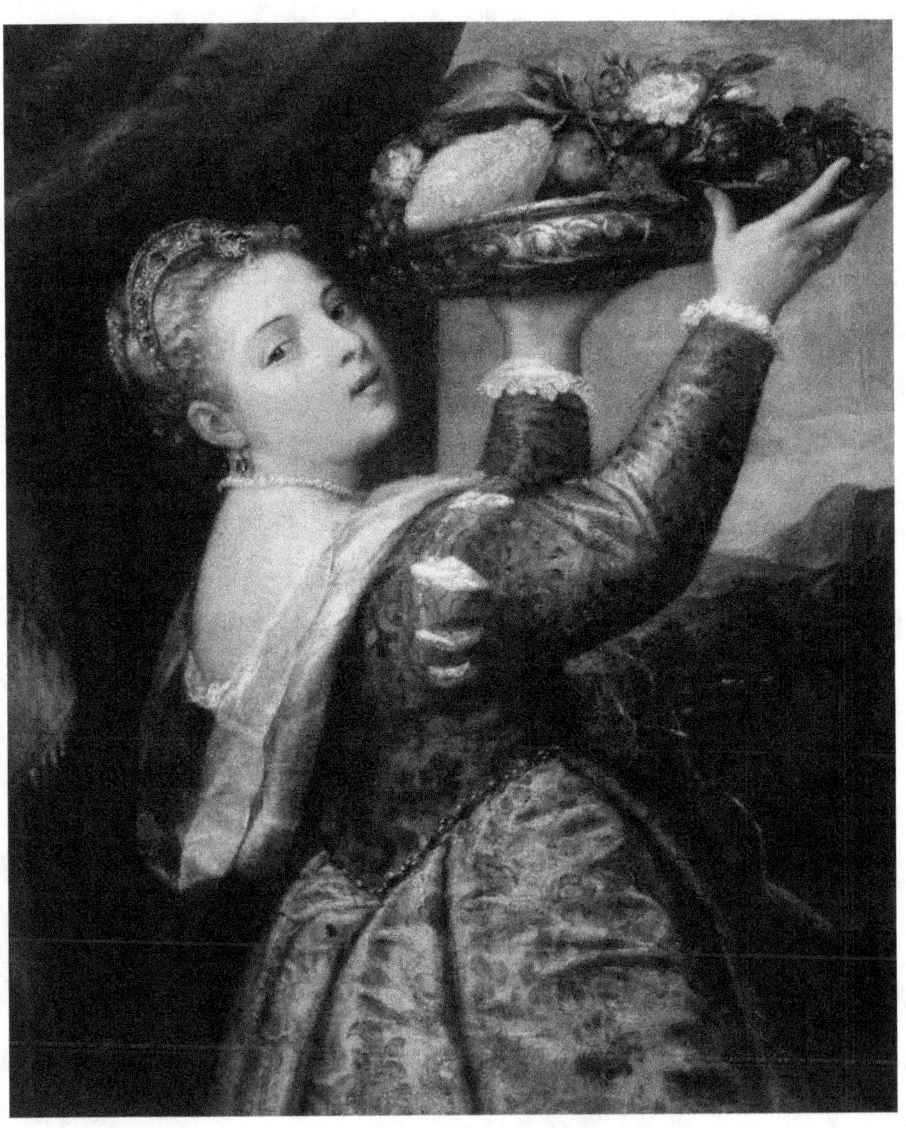

Titian, Girl With a Platter of Fruit, c. 1555, Berlin

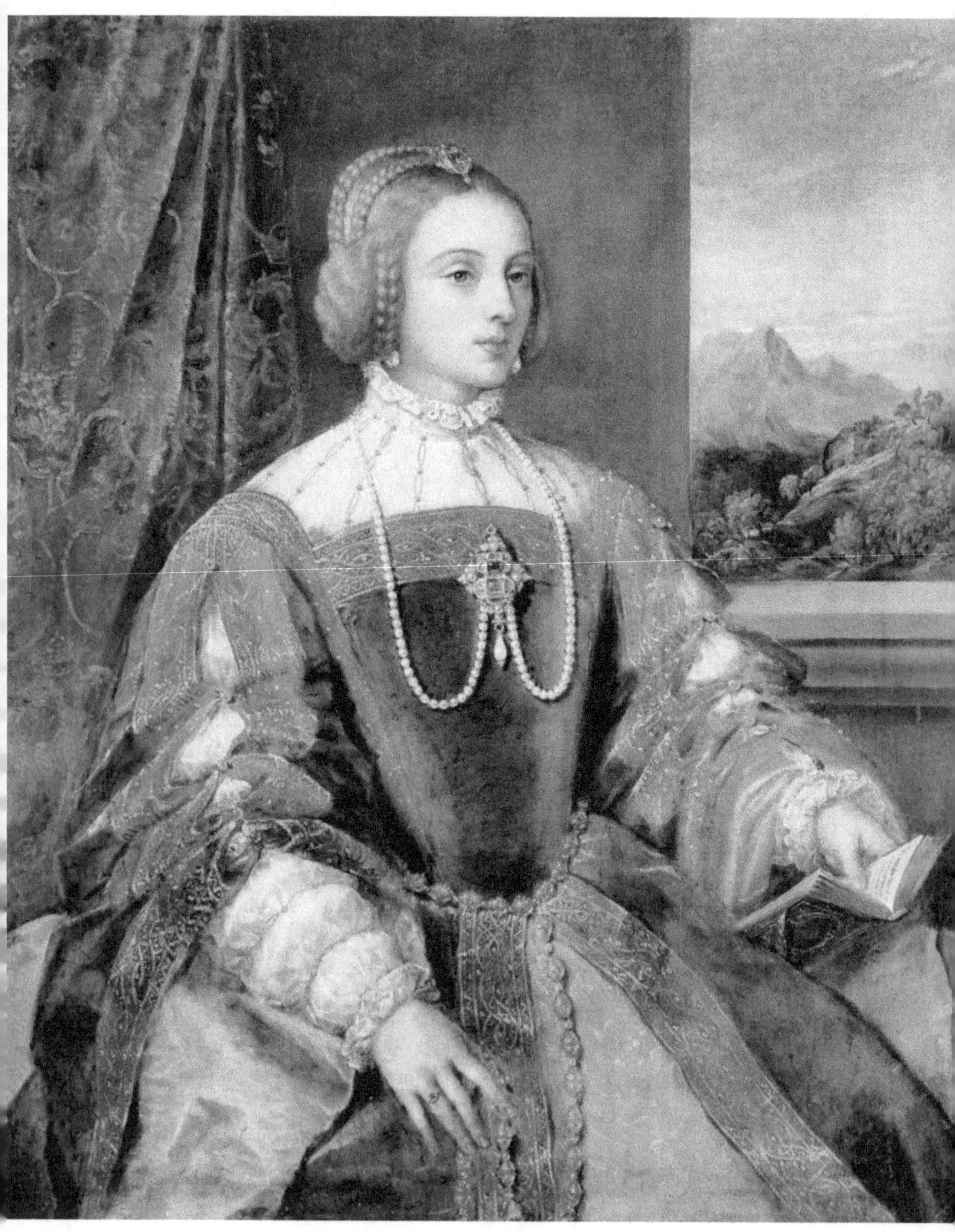

Titian, Portrait of Isabella of Portugal, 1548, Prado

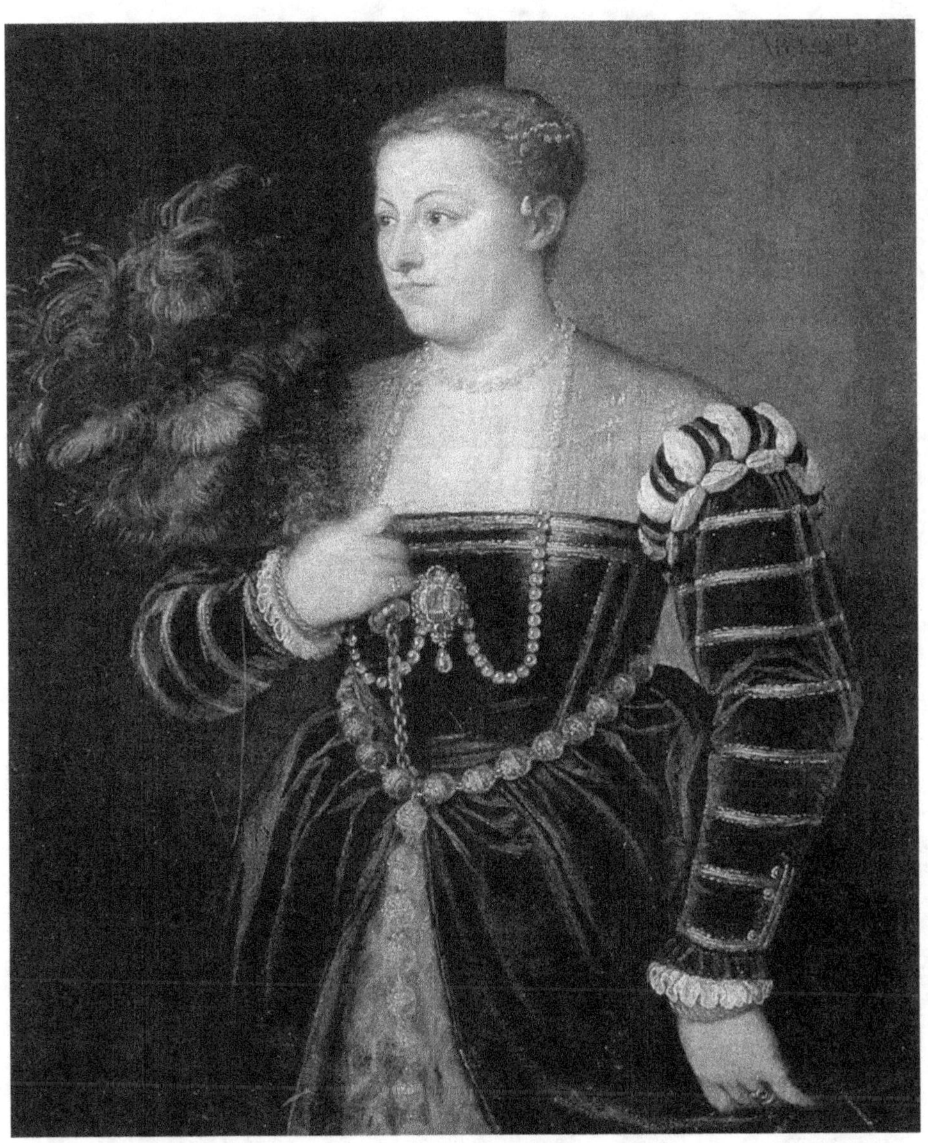

Titian, Lavinia, 1560-65

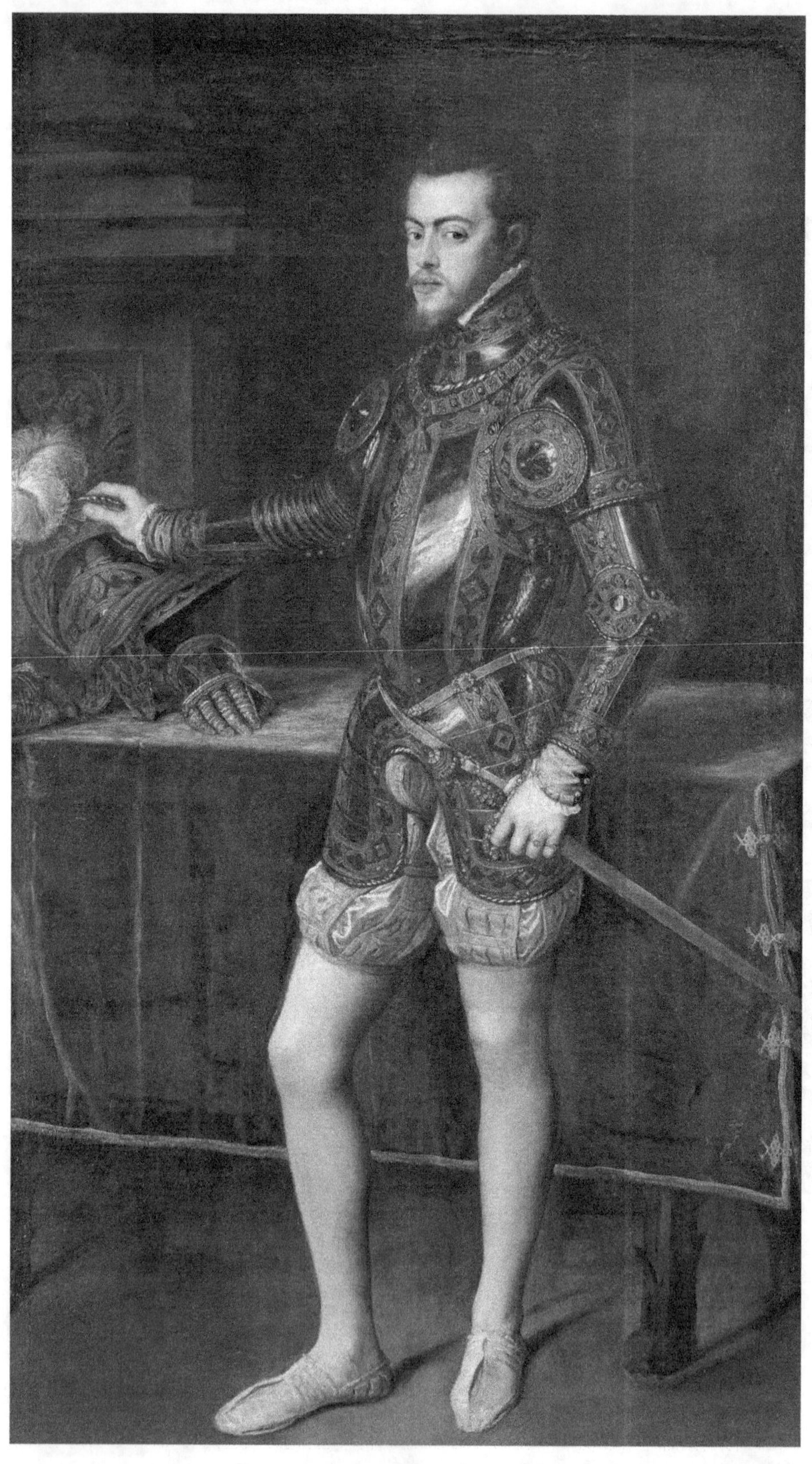

Titian, Philip II, 1551, Prado, Madrid

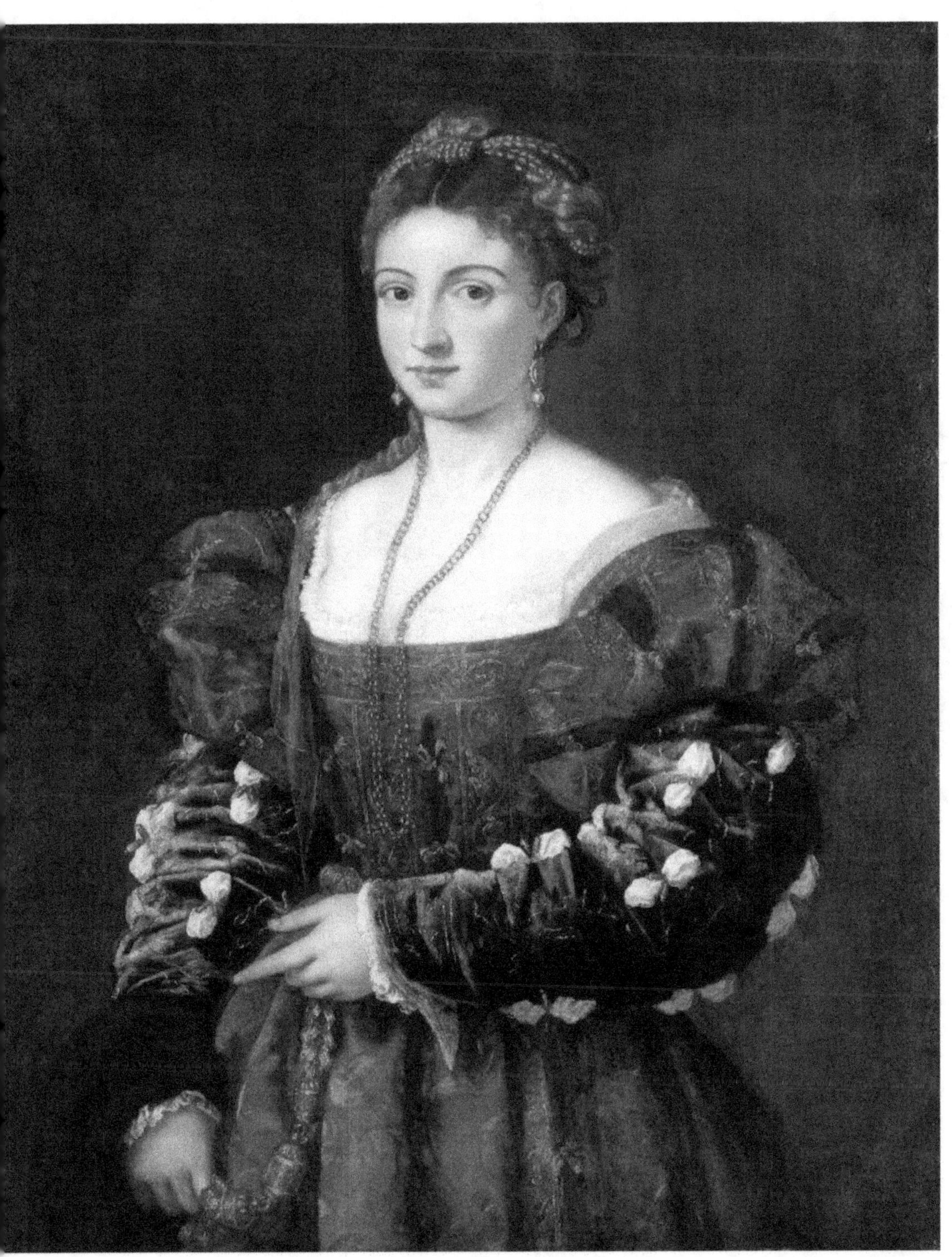

Titian, The Bella, 1536, Pitti Palace

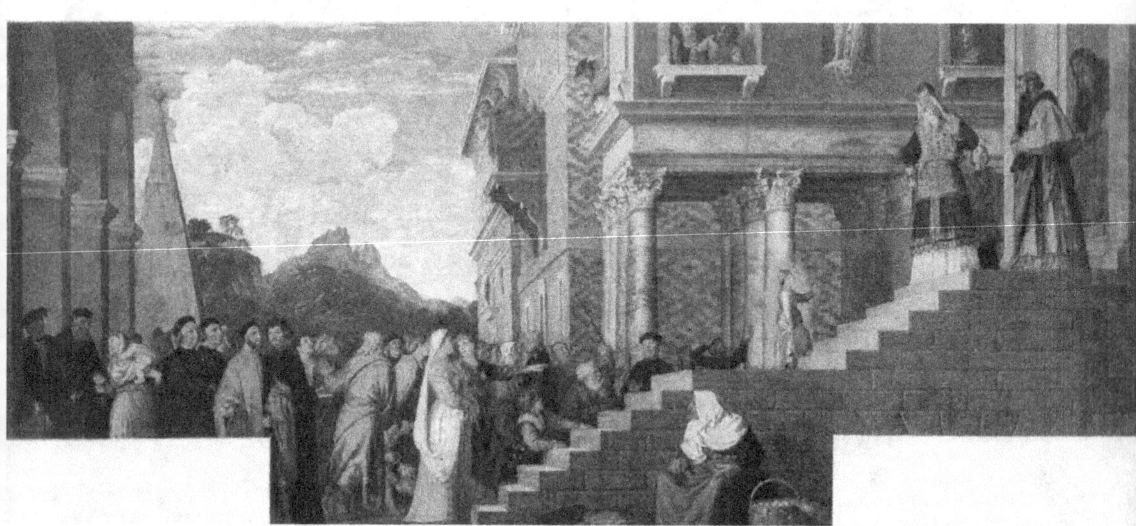

Titian, The Presentation of the Virgin, 1534-38, Venice

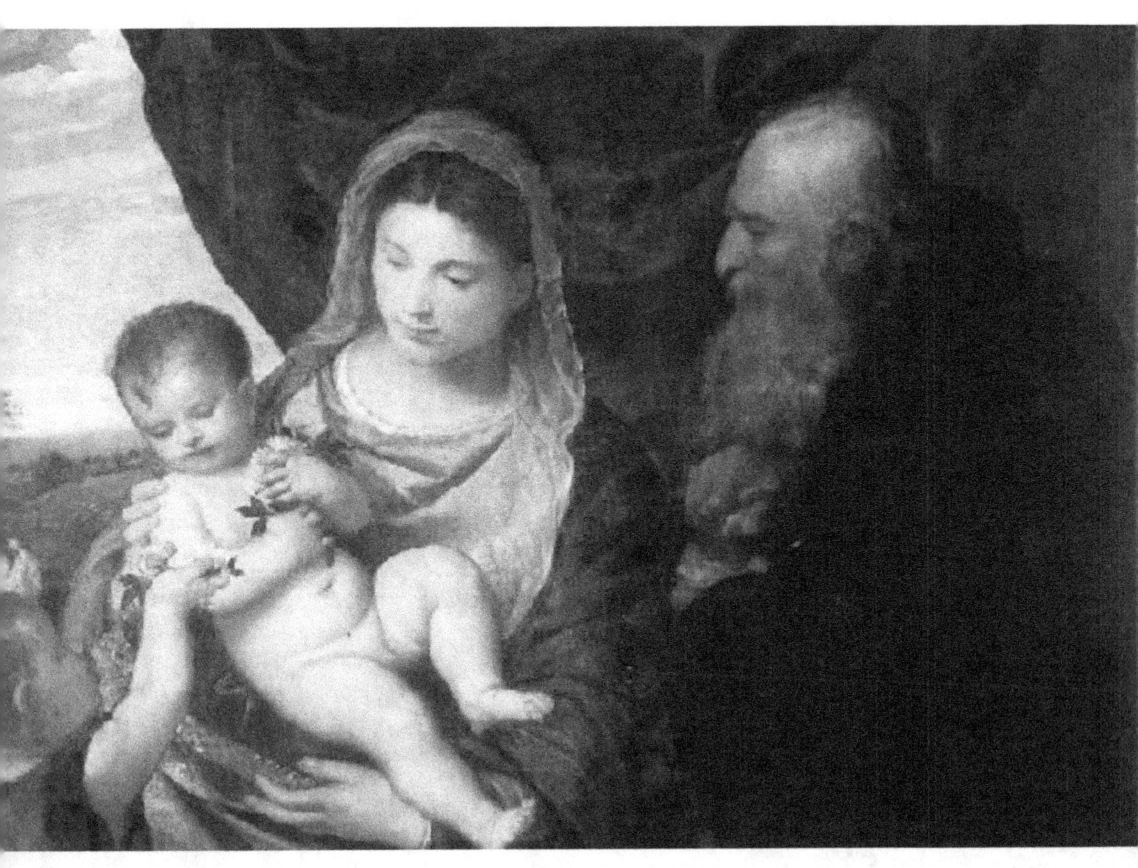

Titian, The Holy Family, 1530s, Uffizi

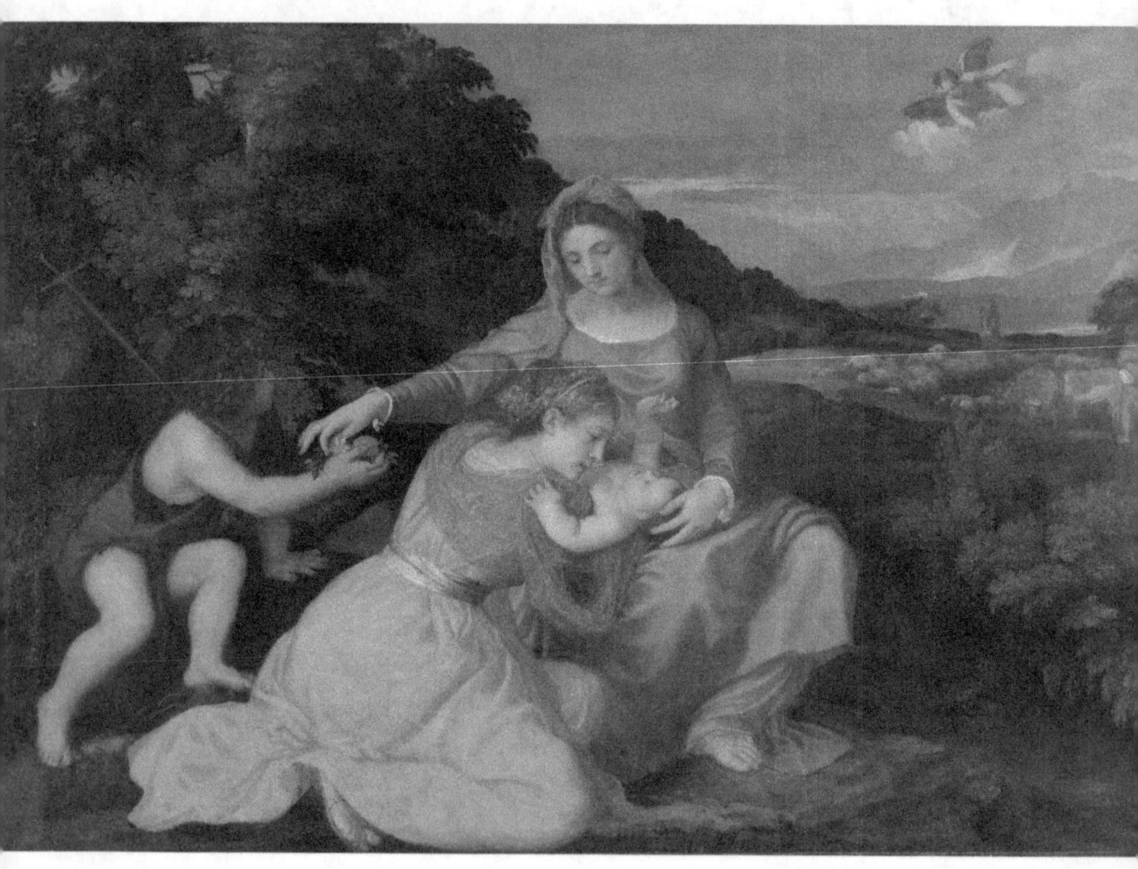

Titian, The Aldobrandini Madonna, National Gallery, London

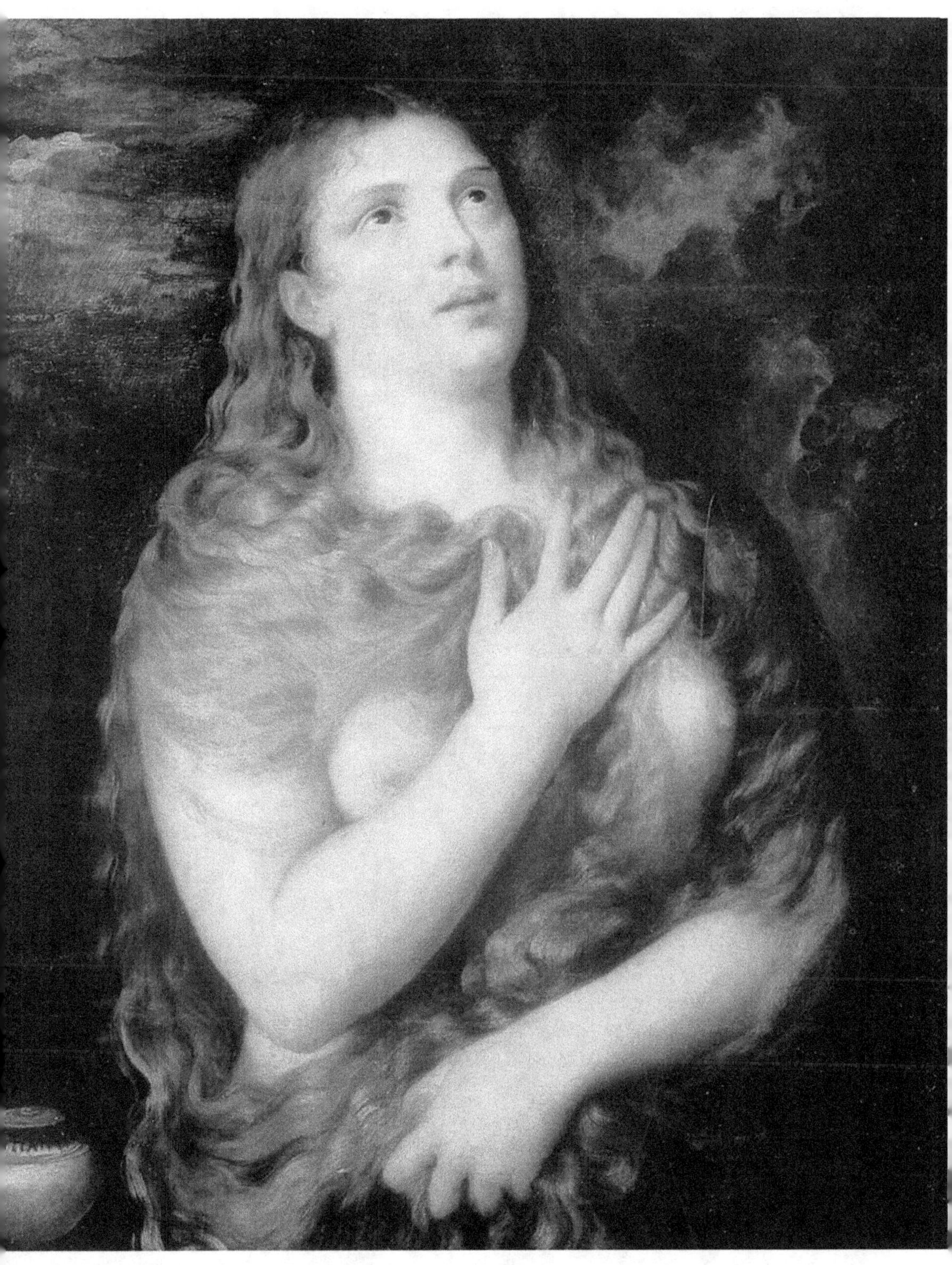

Titian, Mary Magdalene, 1533, Pittit Palace, Florence

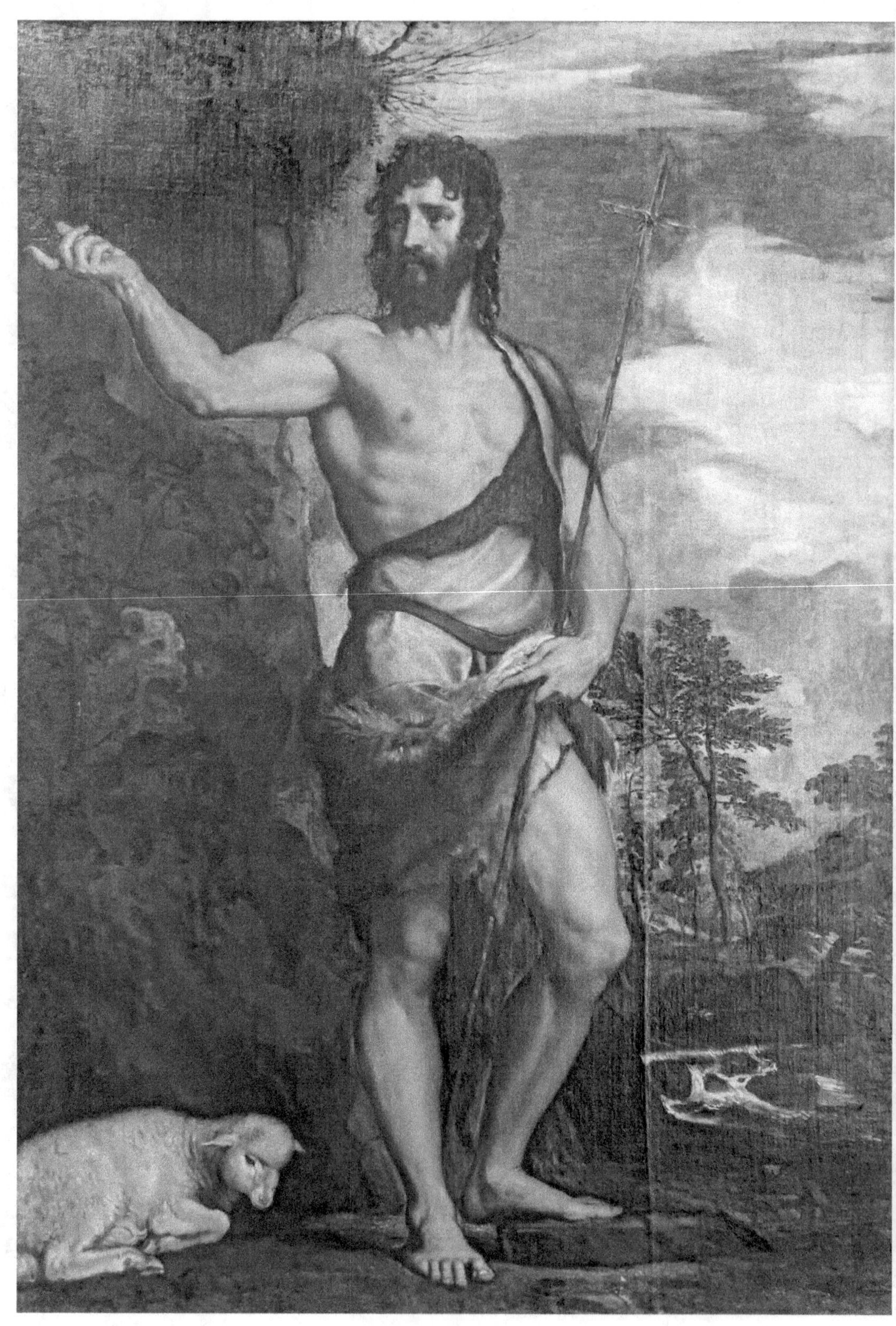

Titian, John the Baptist, 1542, Venice

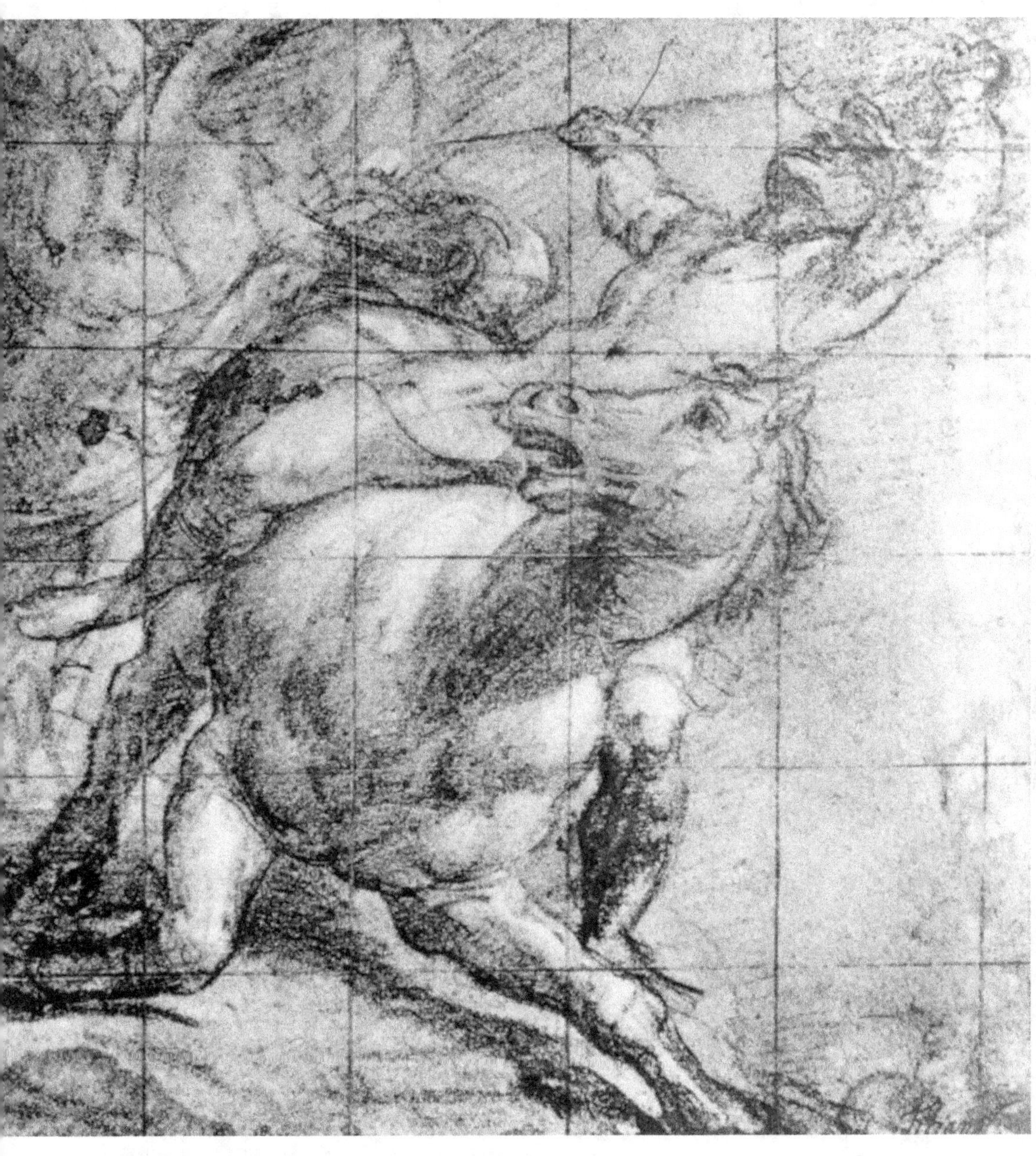

Titian, Studio per cavallo e cavaliere, 1537, Ashmolean Museum, Oxford

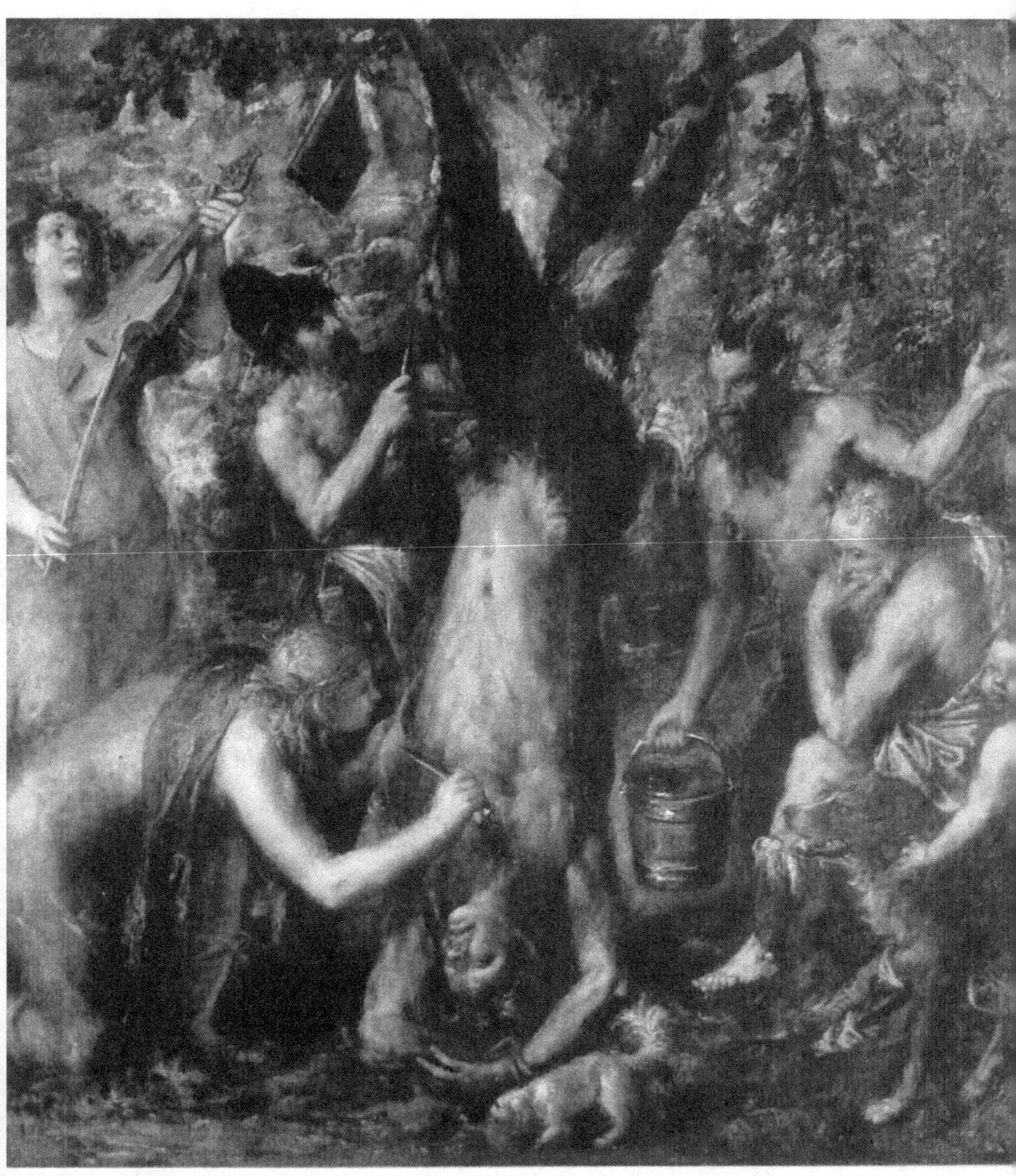

Titian, The Flaying of Marsyas, c. 1570-76, Kromeriz,

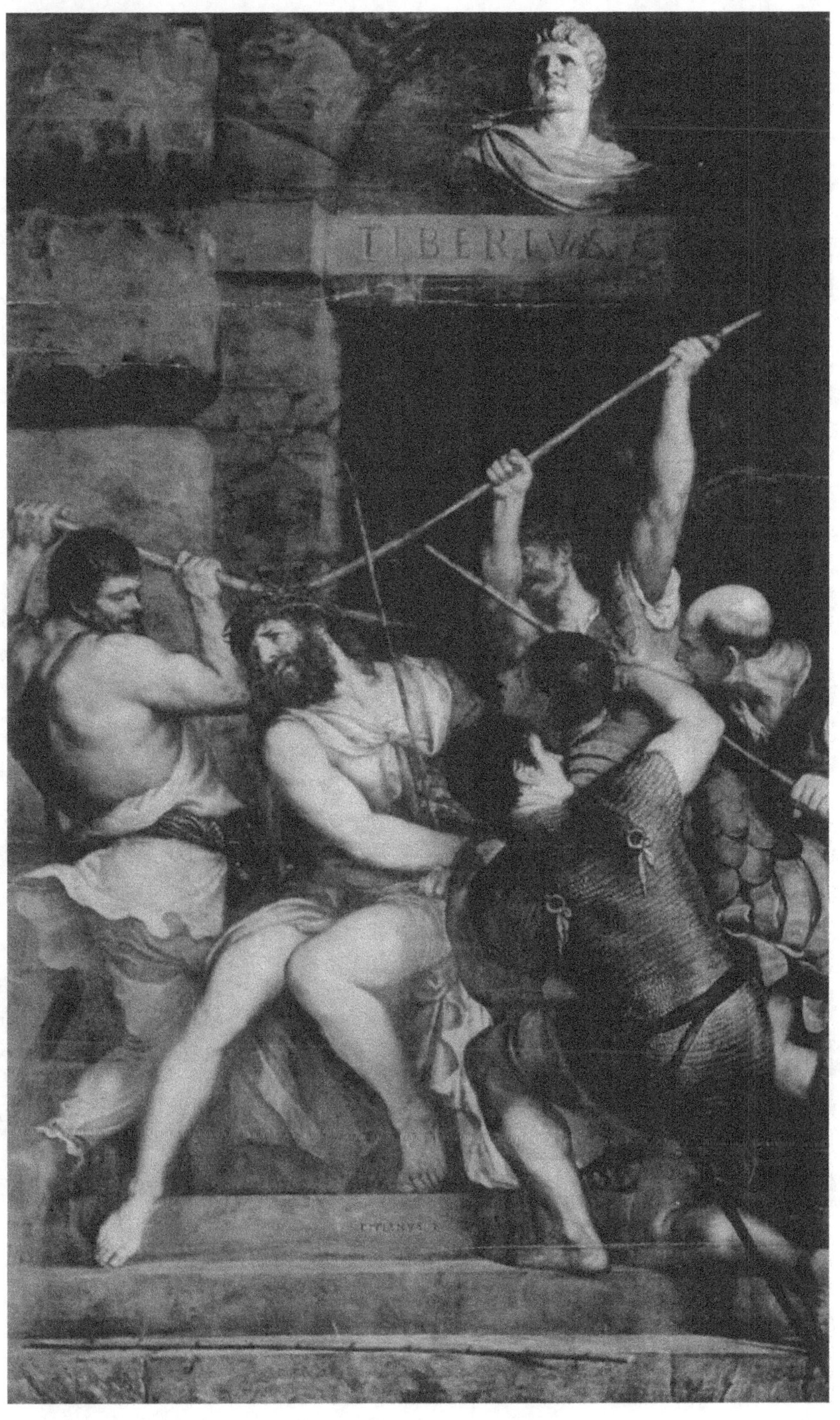

Titian, The Crowning With Thorns, 1572-76, Munich

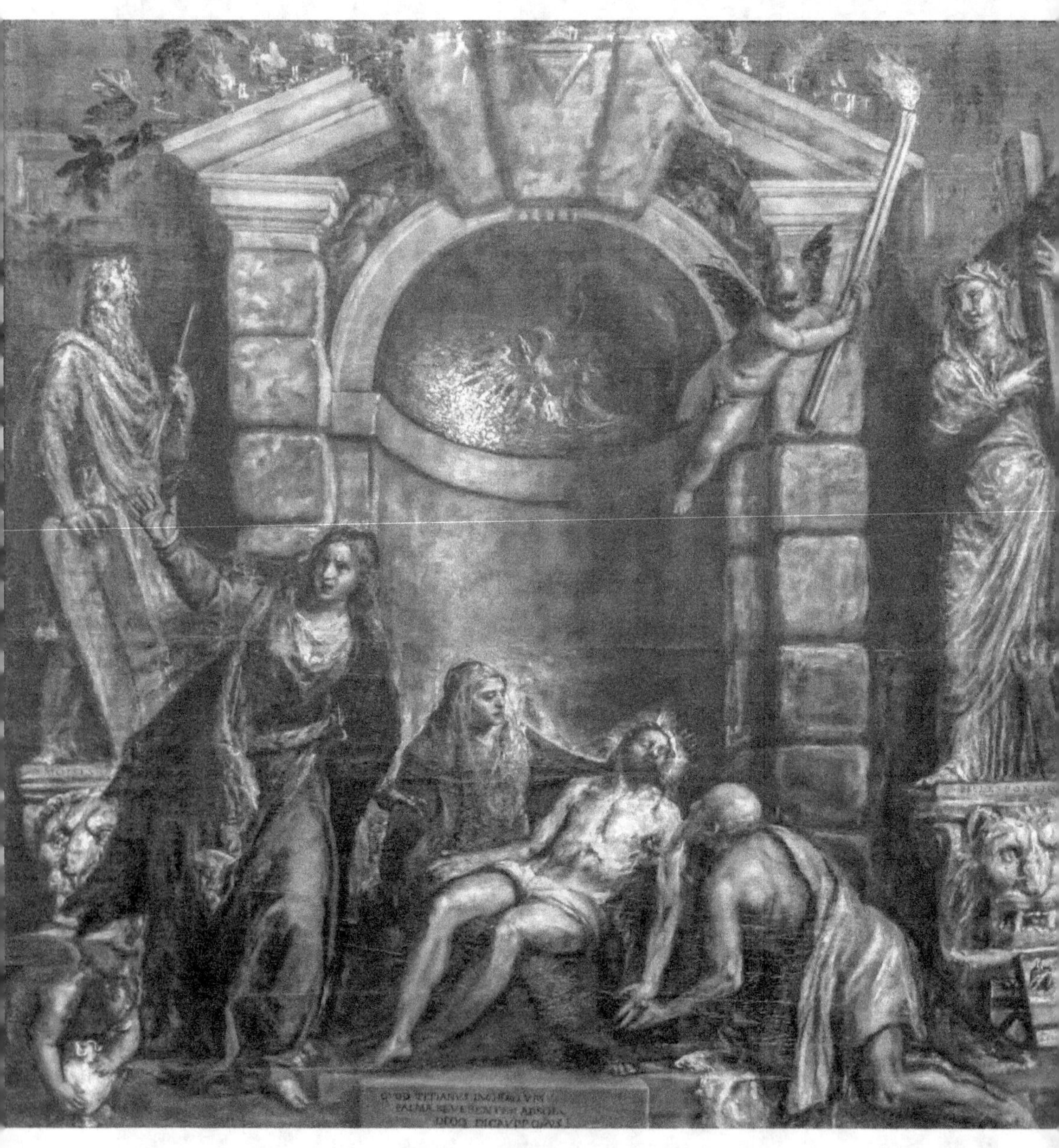

Titian, Pietà, 1576, Venice

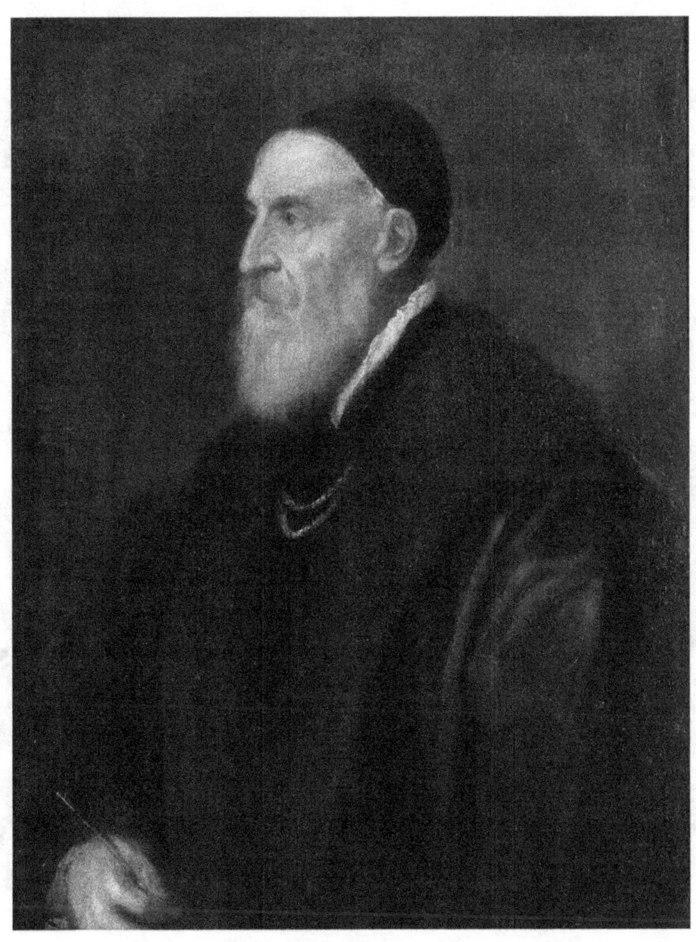

Titian, Self-Portrait, 1565, Prado, Madrid

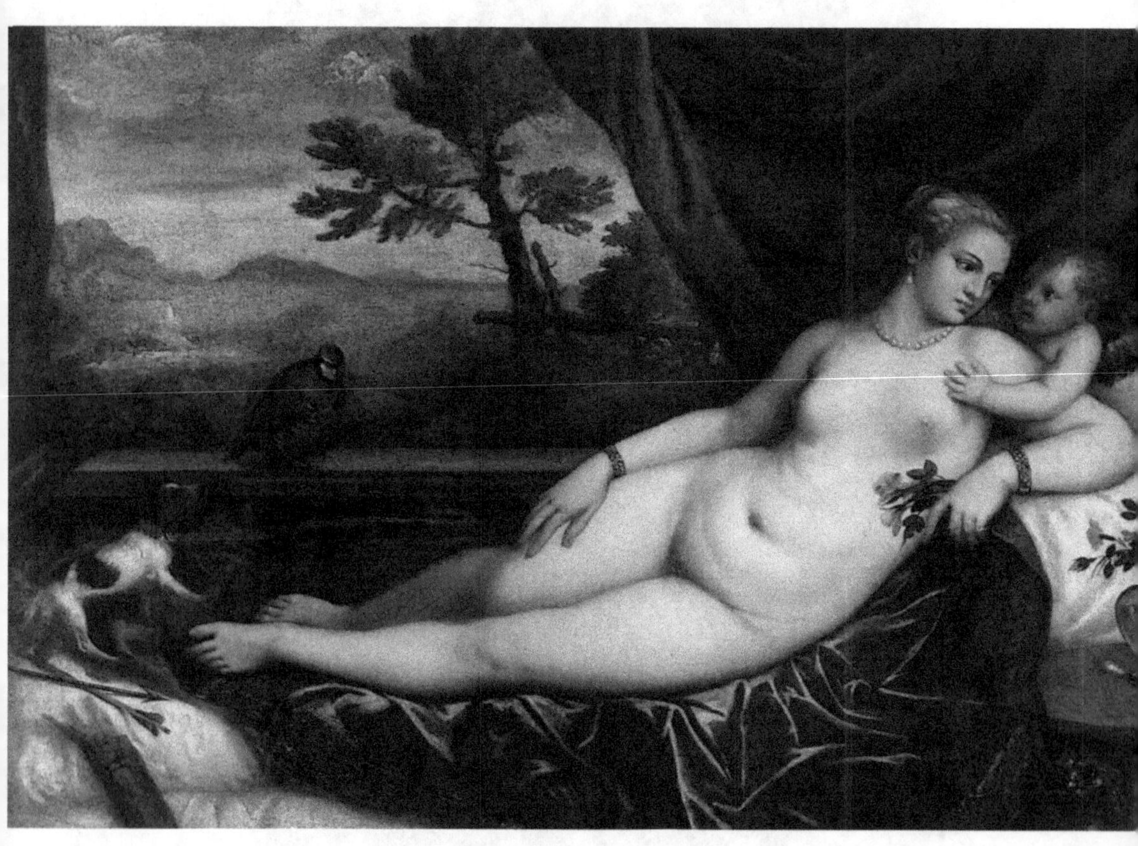

Titian, Venus and Cupid, 1550, Uffizi

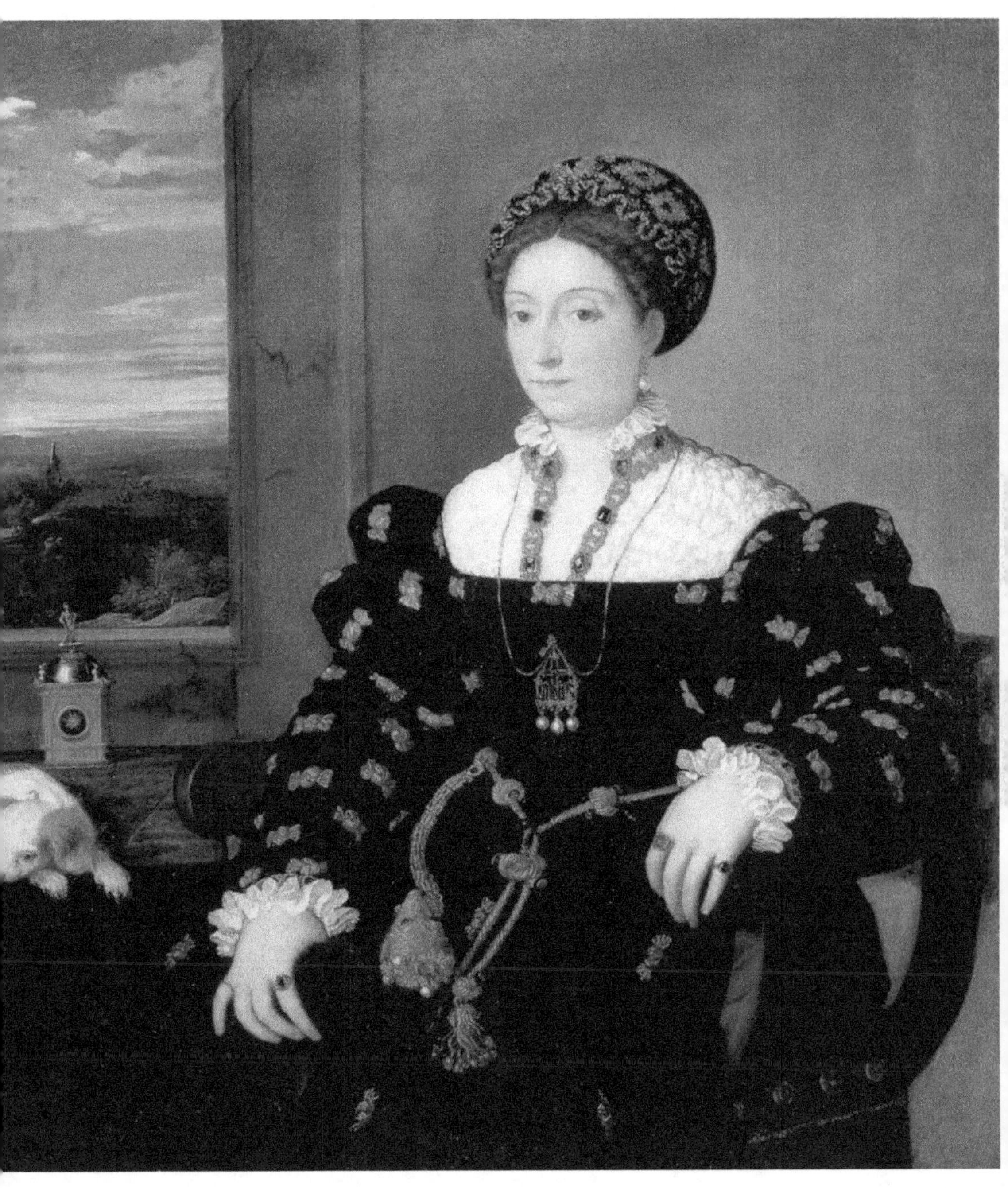

Titian, Portrait of Eleonora Gonzaga, 1538, Uffizi

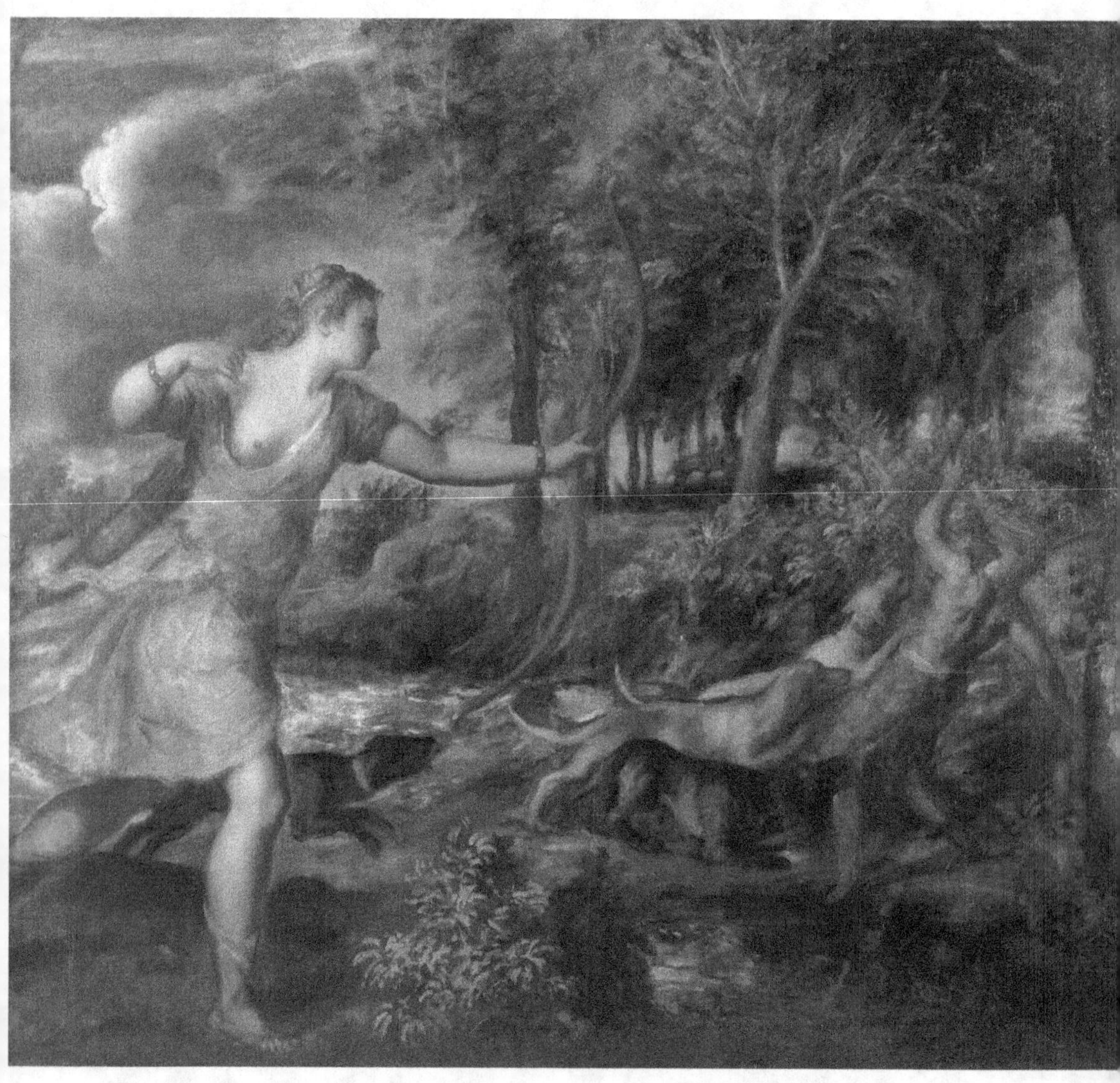

Titian, The Death of Actaeon 1559-75
National Gallery, London

III

THE LAST DECADES

Titian's last work for Charles V. was the famous "Gloria." This was painted at a time when Charles had decided to end his days in the shadow of the Church, and is to be seen to-day in the Prado, a composition of amazing strength and wonderful inspiration. The Father and the Son are seen enthroned, with the Virgin Mary at the feet of Christ, and the Patriarchs grouped in the background. Charles himself in his shroud is pleading for forgiveness, an angel by his side encourages him and supports his appeal. The lighting of the picture is masterly, and so impressed the Emperor that he took it with him into retirement, and directed that it should be placed above his tomb.

Philip II. has no enviable reputation in this country, but his position as patron of the arts stands far above criticism. Though he was a sober ascetic upon whom the authority of the Church weighed very heavily, he did not ask Titian to devote himself entirely to religious pictures. In matters of art he saw his way to making a considerable concession to the spirit of the Renaissance, and when he took over the burden of empire he commissioned several mythological subjects from the old painter. Among them were the "Venus and Adonis" now in the Prado, the "Diana surprised by Actaeon" in Bridge-water House, and the "Jupiter and Antiope" in the Louvre. The allegorical pictures, the latest work of the painter's life, were commissioned later.

Strangely enough the years had done little or nothing to dim the lustre of the painter's work, his colour was still supremely beautiful, his feeling for landscape more intense than it had ever been, while his capacity for striking and novel composition remained a thing to wonder at. Of course Philip was not content with secular subjects, and Titian was required to paint a certain number of pictures for the Escorial, but he is best represented by his mythological subjects. Perhaps they made a more direct appeal to him because by their side the religious pictures were a little old-fashioned, and he does not seem to have faced allegorical subjects with enthusiasm.

It is interesting to turn to Vasari and read some of the things he has to say about the painter at this period of his life, for although the old chronicler is not the most accurate of writers, he is at least a very interesting one and he knew Titian intimately. He says of the famous "Gloria" picture to which reference has been made – "The composition of this work was in accordance with the orders of his Majesty, who was then giving evidence of his intention to retire, as he afterwards did, from mundane affairs, to the end that he might die in the manner of a true Christian, fearing God and labouring for his own salvation." It is not difficult to imagine the emotion that this picture must have roused among those who were privileged to see it, when it came fresh from the painter's studio, to impress an age that had not forgotten to be devout.

Again Vasari says, "In the year 1566 when I, the writer of the present history, was in Venice, I went to visit Titian as one who was his friend, and found him, although then very old, still with the pencils in his hand painting busily." The old gossip goes on to say that Paris Bordone, who "had studied grammar and become an excellent musician," had set himself to imitate Titian, who did not love him on that account, and had sought to keep him from getting commissions. Bordone persevered and went to Augsburg, where he painted pictures, now lost, for some of the great German merchants. This little glimpse of rivalry suggests to us that Titian was jealous of his reputation, although Vasari tells us elsewhere that he was kind and considerate to his contemporaries, and free from uneasiness, because he had gained a fair amount of wealth, his labours having always been well paid. Vasari hints, too, that he kept his brush in hand too long; he must have written this when he remembered that, for all his many excellences, Titian was a Venetian. "Titian has always been healthy and happy," he writes; "he has been favoured beyond the lot of most men, and has received from Heaven only favours and blessings. In his house he has always been visited by whatever princes, literati, or men of distinction have gone to Venice, for in addition to his excellence in art he has always distinguished himself by courtesy, goodness, and rectitude." Perhaps his remark that Titian's reputation would have stood higher if he had finished work earlier may be no more than a veiled comment upon the indiscriminate misuse of the labours of pupils.

In the latter years of his sojourn in Venice the artist lived in a house towards Murano, between the Church of San Giovanni de Paolo and the Church of the Jesuits. He entertained very largely, giving supper parties from which no seasonable delicacy was lacking, and gathering round him distinguished men and women who were far less celebrated for their morals than for their attractions. His gossip Aretino was generally of the party, and it is to him that we owe so much of our intimate knowledge of the painter's home life and troubles. Aretino's death in 1556 must have been a great blow to Titian.

Vasari tells us that the painter's income was considerable. Charles V. paid a thousand gold crowns for every portrait of himself and, when he conferred the patent of nobility upon the painter, he accompanied it with an annual gift of two hundred crowns. Philip II., son of the great Emperor, added another two hundred annually, the German merchants gave him three hundred, so that he had seven hundred crowns a year without taking into account the commissions that came to him on every side, and, as he was painting for the richest and most generous people of his generation, his annual income must have been very considerable. And yet Titian's own correspondence, of which a part has been preserved, shows that the State grants were not always paid regularly. It is of course far more easy for an arbitrary ruler to make gifts to his favourites than it is for the State Treasury to respond to the demands that must needs follow each grant, and Spanish finances have always been difficult to administer.

As he grew older and his hand lost part at least of its cunning, Titian depended more and more upon pupils, but in this he was only following the custom of his time. It is said that a clever German artist, who worked in his studio, was responsible for the greater part of several of the later pictures. The Council of Ten though they had taken from him the office of Painter of Doges and had given it to Tintoretto, offered him a commission in the late 'sixties; even if they had a grievance against him they could not afford to nourish it. Then again if Titian was not always prompt in doing the work for which he was paid, even if he employed pupils to a greater extent than seemed necessary to those who had to pay for the finished canvas, it must have been hard to quarrel with him, for his personality would seem to have been most engaging. He was an excellent musician as well as a good host, Paolo Veronese has included him in the famous "Marriage in Cana" (Louvre) playing a double bass. Moreover Titian was a courtier whose correspondence, although it dealt so largely with matter of finance, lacks none of the stilted graces of the time, and these may have helped to conciliate angry patrons. He seems to have been an affectionate father, and if he had any besetting sin it was love of money, his anxiety in this respect being increased by the fact that he was not always able to collect the accounts due to him. Yet he saved enough to buy land round his birthplace and it is reported that he went to Cadore whenever he had the opportunity. Clearly an appreciative sense of the perennial peace of the Dolomites never left him.

By his wife, to whom he was not married until two sons had been born, Titian had four children of whom two grew up. Pomponio, to whom we have referred, was the eldest; and he came to a bad end, being a dissipated man. Orazio, who was the second son, became a painter. One daughter died young, and there was another, Lavinia, portraits of whom may be seen at Dresden and Berlin. His great friends were Pietro Aretino, poet and gossip, who laid half Europe under contribution, and was almost as unscrupulous as he was clever, and the sculptor Sansovino.

Whatever Titian's faults were as a man, they may fairly be forgotten in his merits as an artist, and it is not the least of these merits that he worked from the time when he was a boy to the hour when his brush seemed falling from his hands, unsparing in his devotion to his task. He has left a legacy to the civilised world that compels a measure of admiration equal to that which is paid to Velazquez. Titian was the supreme master of colour, but, unfortunately, few of his pictures have escaped the restorer's hand, and a great many have been damaged in their journeys from city to city in an age when the art of picture packing was still unknown. Exposure to all sorts of weather, long periods of neglect, careless restoration, and reckless repainting would have been enough to destroy the reputation of most painters, but Titian's work has not suffered to the extent that might have been expected. Enough remains of the master to make us not a little envious of the happy patrons of the arts who knew his work in all its glory.

It is hard to say when Titian's life would have come to an end in the ordinary course of events, but it is not unreasonable to suppose that he would have lived to be a centenarian had he retired from Venice when he was ninety and gone to live in Pieve, the well-beloved city that gave him birth. But he would not leave his workshop, and in 1575 the plague paid another visit to Venice. It will be remembered that soon after the League of Cambrai when Titian was in Padua, a visitation had devastated Venice and carried off Giorgione among thousands of lesser men. The Venetians were never free from fear of the plague's return. In 1575 the hand of the plague lay heavy upon the City of Lagoons, where sanitation was unknown, and isolation and disinfection were not practised properly. Historians tell us that some 40,000 people perished, the greatest panic prevailed, and while the plague was at its height Titian died. If his own insinuation of the year of his birth be correct he must have been in his ninety-ninth year, but even if we accept the date given by those who believe that he was born as late as 1482, he would have been within seven years of his centenary. The epidemic is recorded in the famous Church of the Redentore on the Giudecca, dedicated to Christ by the Doge Mocenigo, whose portrait painted by Tintoretto may be seen in the Accademia to-day.

In spite of the distress prevailing in the city some effort was made to give the great painter a State funeral, but under the conditions existing, it was impossible to carry out the programme, and he was buried with comparatively little ceremony in the great Church of the Frari which, in addition to having one of the finest works of his hand, is further enriched by the famous altar-piece by his old master Gian Bellini. They say that his residence was entered shortly after his death by some of the riff-raff of Venice, to whom the plague had given a welcome measure of licence, and was despoiled of many of its treasures. Doubtless the painter's house held much that was worth the small risk involved in an hour when the authorities were hardly able to cope with duties to the sick and the disposal of the dead.

In considering the life of Titian we see that much good-fortune went to its making. He was born at the best period of the Renaissance, he was the inheritor of the freedom for which other painters had striven. He painted a world that was as new to artists as were the far-off realms to the Spanish adventurers who were discovering new countries and new trade routes, and paving the way for the ultimate decline of Venice. At the outset of his career Titian's work was full of the joy of life, it was the expression of an age that seemed to have come of age, of a city that had turned to canvas and marble rather than to books for a reflection of the new life. While the painter progressed, overcoming the various difficulties of expression that confronted him, making daring and successful experiments in composition, handling colour as it had never been handled before, this feeling of enthusiasm that belonged to the age was expressed in all his work. Then again he had the great advantage of claiming for sitters the most distinguished men of his time, the statesmen and rulers who were making history at the expense of the map of Europe, the men who held spiritual or temporal power, and the women they delighted to honour. Naturally enough these conditions gave added scope to the painter's talent; and his subjects were worthy of his brush. He could seek out what was best and most characteristic in his sitters, and express through the medium of his art not only the likeness but the personality underlying it. Had his work been more fortunate, had it been preserved in anything like its entirety, we should be able to read the history of his times in a clearer light, for though the written word can tell us much, the cleverly wrought picture has still more to say, and we can rely upon canvas, if Titian painted it, to refute or to confirm the verdict of the historian.

Happily, too, Titian's art grew with his age. Practice and experience ripened it, and some of his finest pictures were painted when he was past the span of life that the Psalmist has allotted to man. He covered every field, no form of painting seems to have come amiss to him. Altar-pieces, portraits, historical pictures, mythological and allegorical subjects, one and all claimed his attention from time to time, and though we are all entitled to express our preference, there will be few to say that he failed in any style of work. Perhaps he was least successful in allegorical subjects, and in the portraits of women, but, if this be so, his failure is merely relative, he attained such heights in mythological subjects and men's portraits, that the other work is not so good by comparison. If he gave us no picture devoted entirely to landscape it is worth remarking that the appeal of nature was an ever growing one. The impression given him by the mountains round Cadore was never lost. From the time when he completed Gian Bellini's last picture down to the time when the plague came to Venice and found him with an unfinished picture on his easel, the attraction of the countryside he knew so well was always with him, and he lost no opportunity of expressing it. Gian Bellini had opened the walls that shut in the Madonna and the Saints of the earlier masters, he had given the world glimpses of exquisite landscape through which the romance woven round his figures seemed to spread. Titian opened the gates still further, giving a larger, wider, and more splendid view, convincing his contemporaries and successors that landscape could never more be overlooked.

He would seem to have made few studies, a sketch by Titian is one of the rarest things in art, he did not see in line but in colour. With Titian as with Velazquez after him it is hard to separate colour from line, and in colour he was the acknowledged master of his own time and the guide of the ages after him. Some of his great contemporaries, not Venetians of course, declared that Titian was a poor draughtsman, but it is well to remember that among the Venetians, art was an affair of painting, among the Florentines it embraced sculpture and architecture; the mere handling of paint, however splendid the results, would not suffice Florentine ambitions. It might even be said that much Florentine painting is little more than tinted drawing. We go to Titian for colour even to-day, when time and exposure and repainting have taken so much from the wealth that he gave to his pictures, and we can see that as he grew to ripe age he sought to obtain his colour effects by less obvious means than those that served him at the outset. It is hard for any but an artist to realise the secret of the cause that produced the later results, but, if it be left for the artist to explain it is easy for the layman to appreciate. With Titian,

Venetian painting reached the zenith of its achievement, after him through Tintoretto and Veronese, the descent is slow but sure, and we are left wondering whether any fresh revival of the world's enthusiasm, any new discovery of the world's youth is destined to bring into art the spirit of enthusiasm that gave a Titian to the world. There are few signs in our own time, but then we do not live in an age of great crises religious or political, or, if we do, we are too near to the changes to recognise them.

Perhaps there are some who find amusement in the suggestion that Titian's action emancipating art from the thraldom of the Church was a great and glorious one, not unattended by danger and difficulties. To these sceptics one can but reply by quoting the decree of the Council of Nicaea dated A.D. 787 and never repealed. Here we find the attitude of Authority towards art set out in plainest fashion. "It is not the invention of the painter which creates a picture," says this remarkable decree, "but the inviolable law and tradition of the Church. It is not the painter but the Holy Fathers who have to invent and dictate. To them manifestly belongs the composition, to the painter only the execution."

A few great artists in later times had made their protest, definite or indefinite, against the attitude of the Church, but Titian rescued art as Perseus rescued Andromeda.

On the following pages are illustrations of some of the contemporaries of Titian.

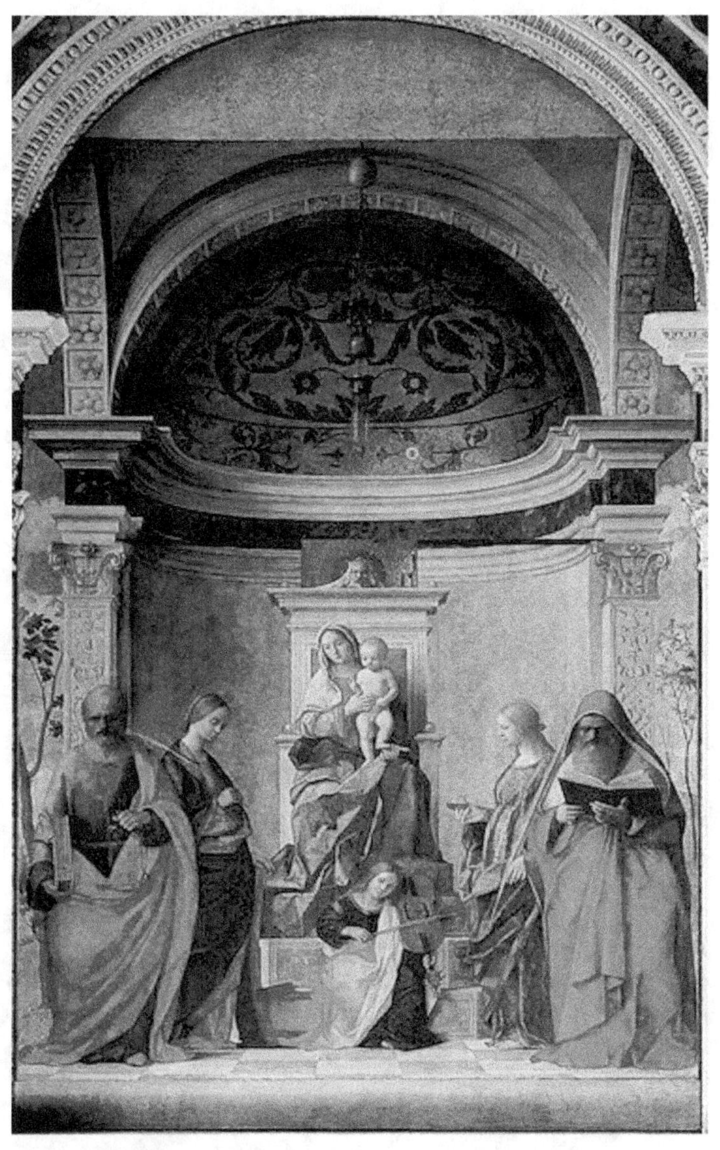

Giovanni Bellini, San Zaccaria Altarpiece

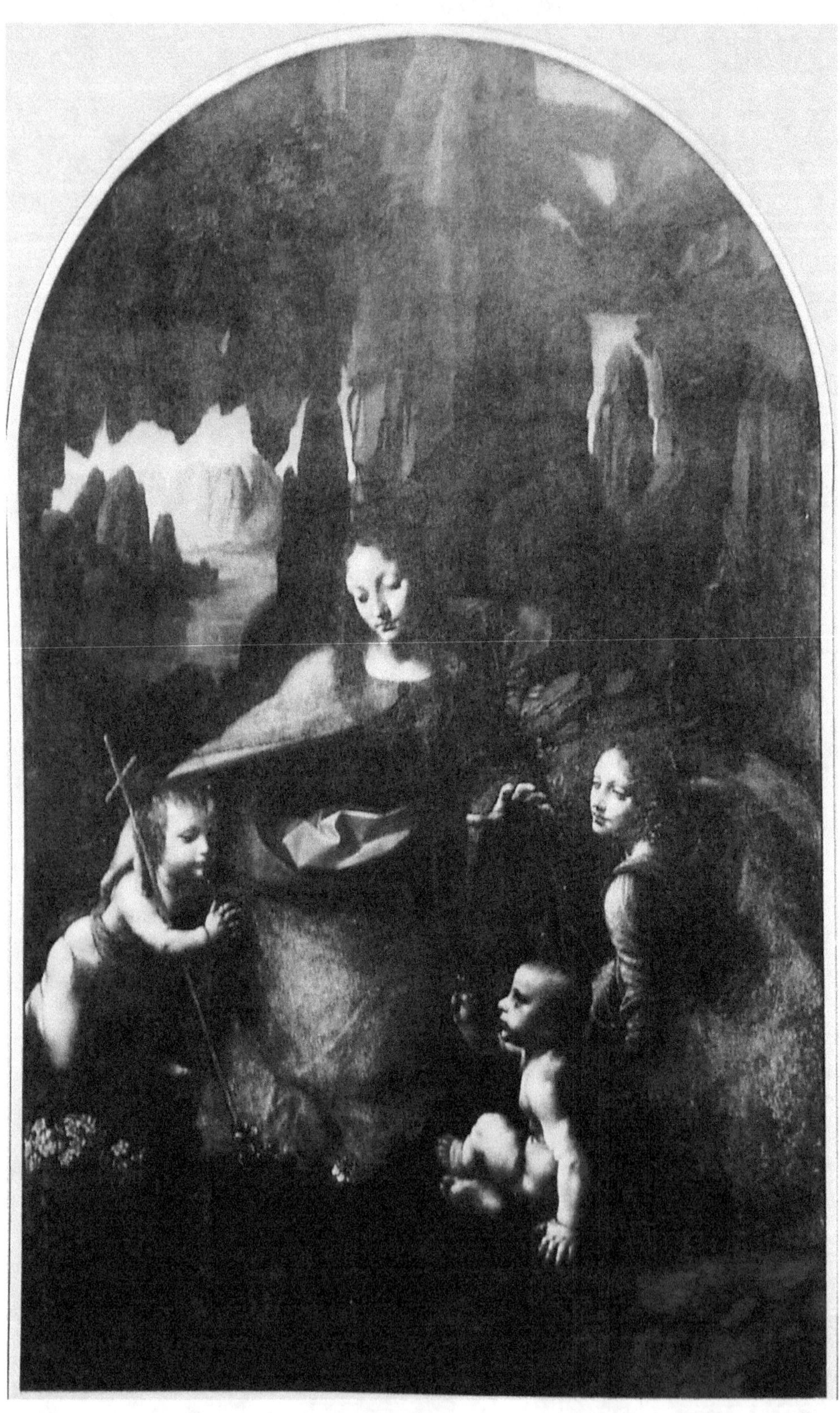

Leonardo da Vinci, *The Virgin of the Rocks*, National Gallery, London

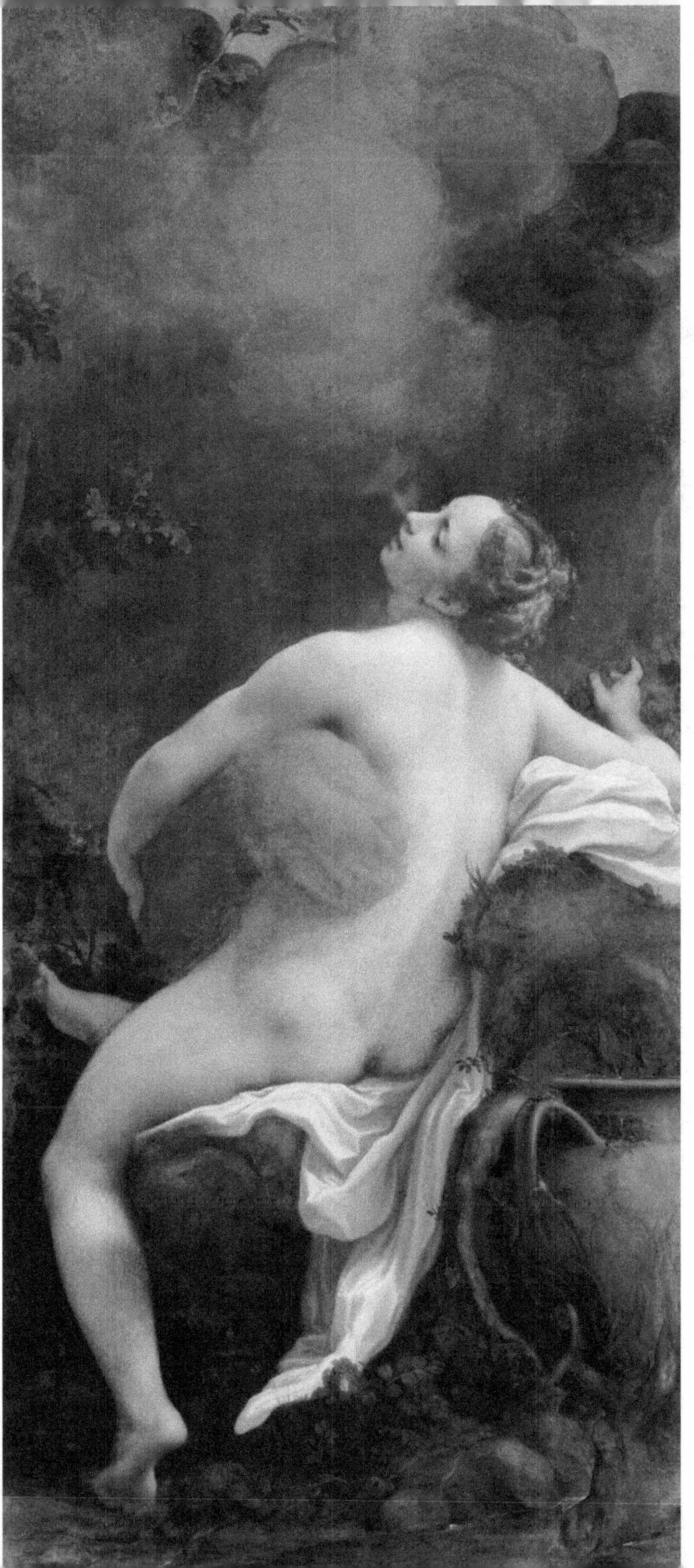

Correggio,
Jupiter and Antiope

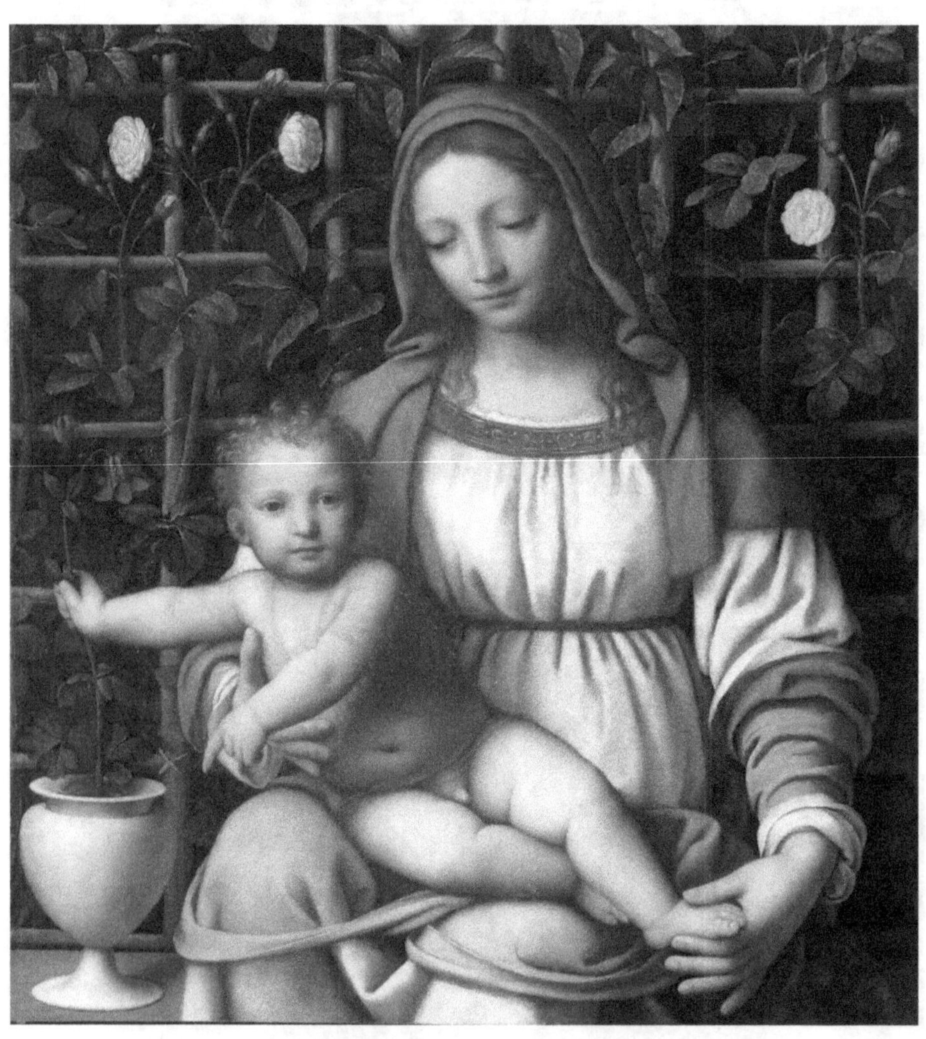

Bernardino Luini, Madonna and Child, Milan

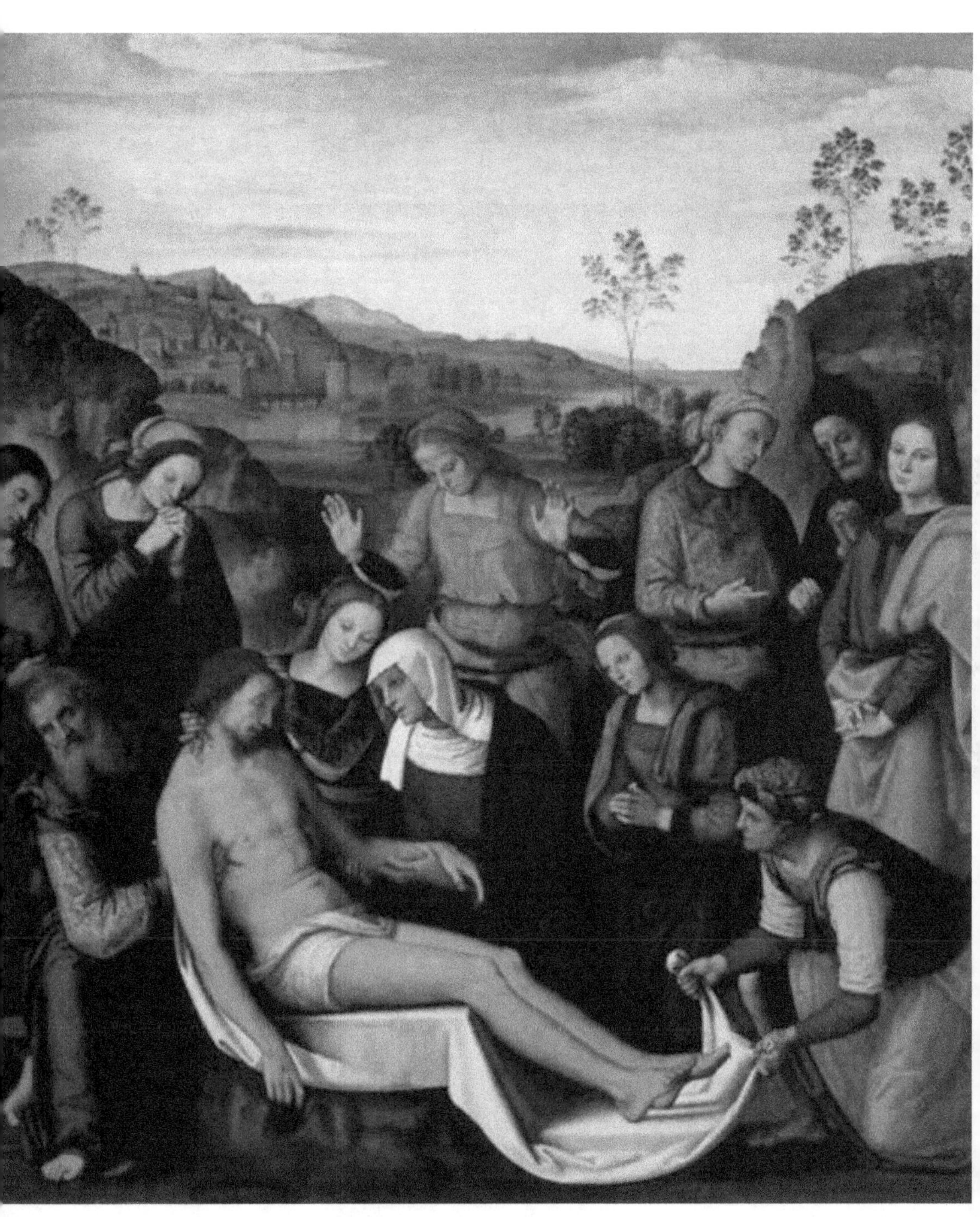

Perugino, The Mourning of the Dead Christ, 1495

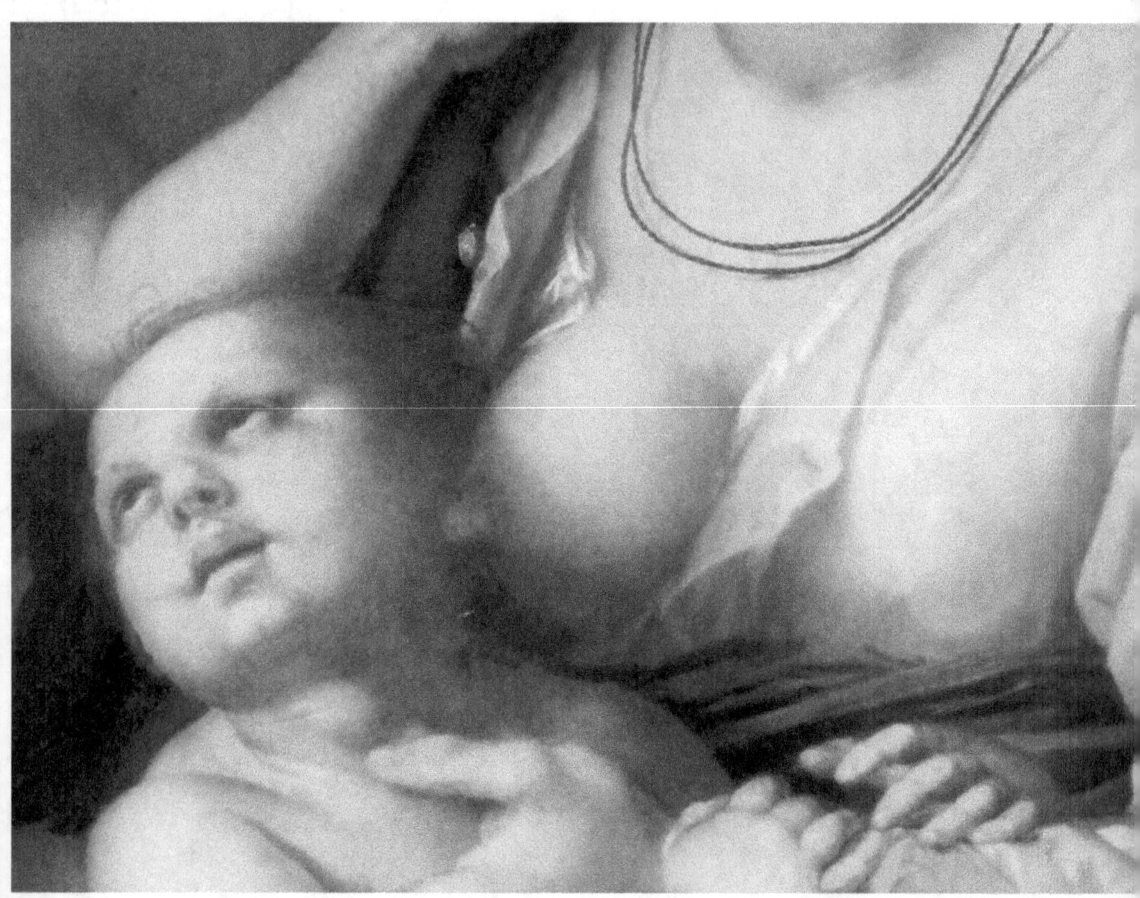

Andrea del Sarto, Madonna and Child, detail

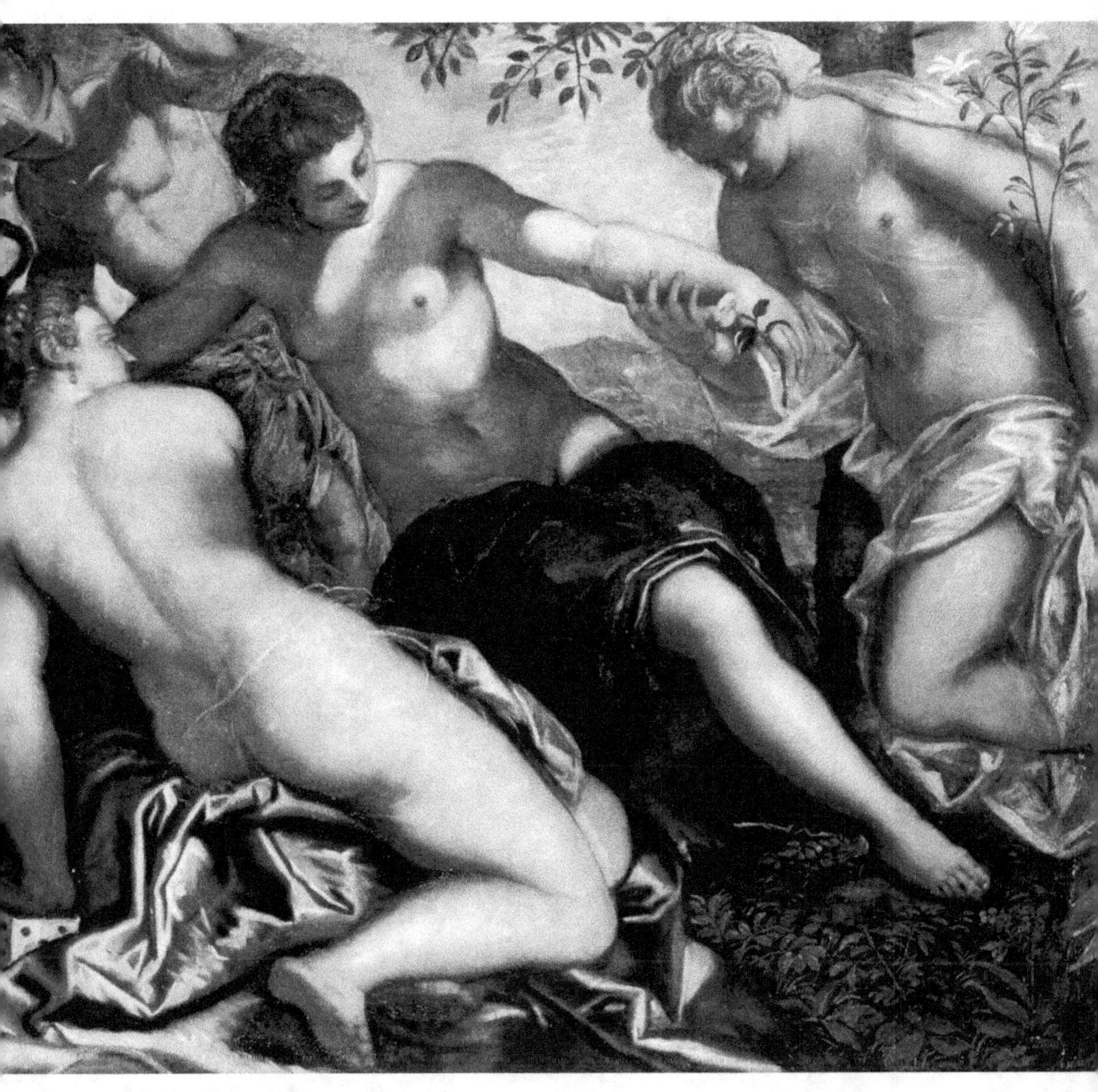

Jacopo Tintoretto, Mercury and the Graces, 1577

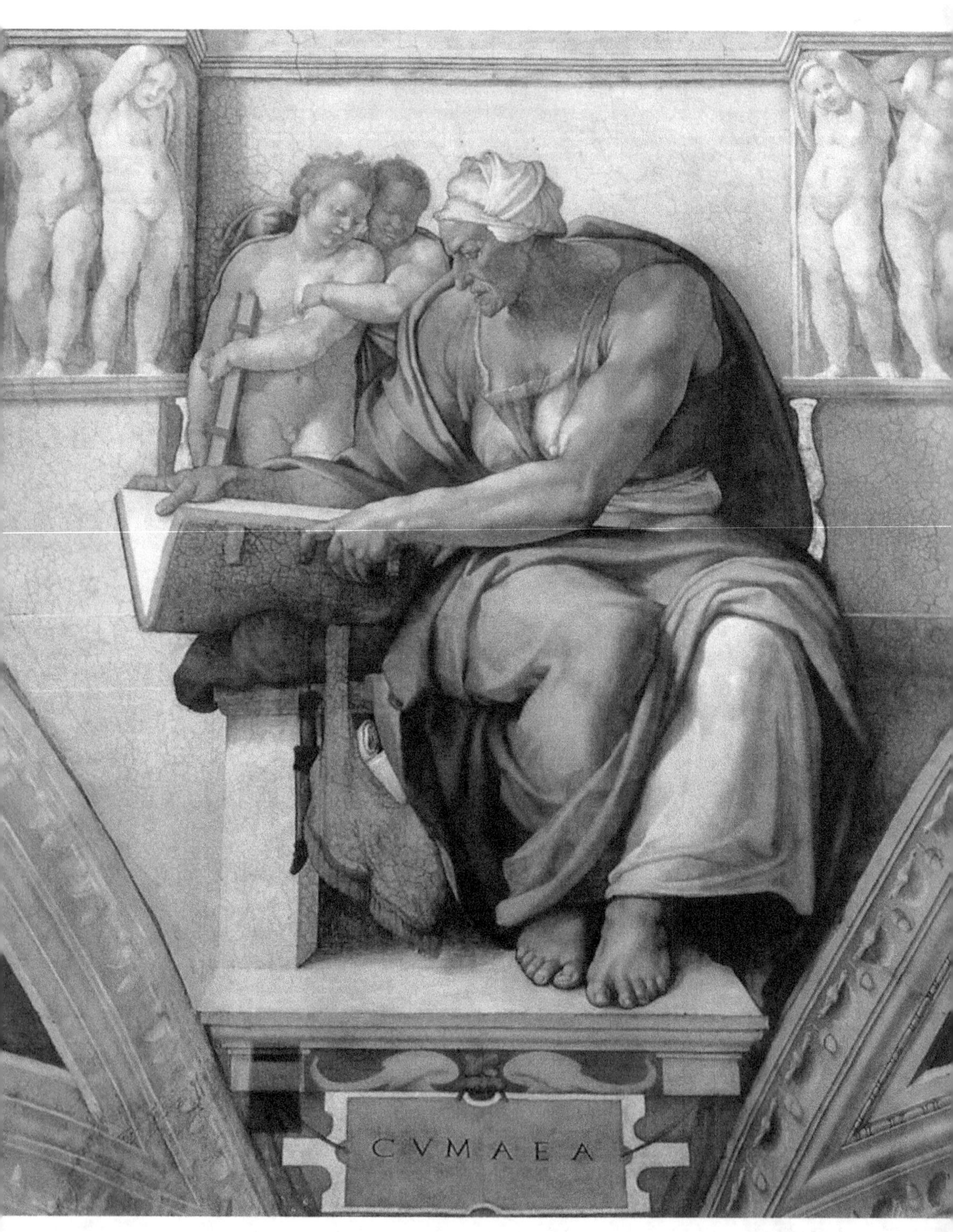

Michelangelo, Cumaean Sibyle, Sistine Chapel.

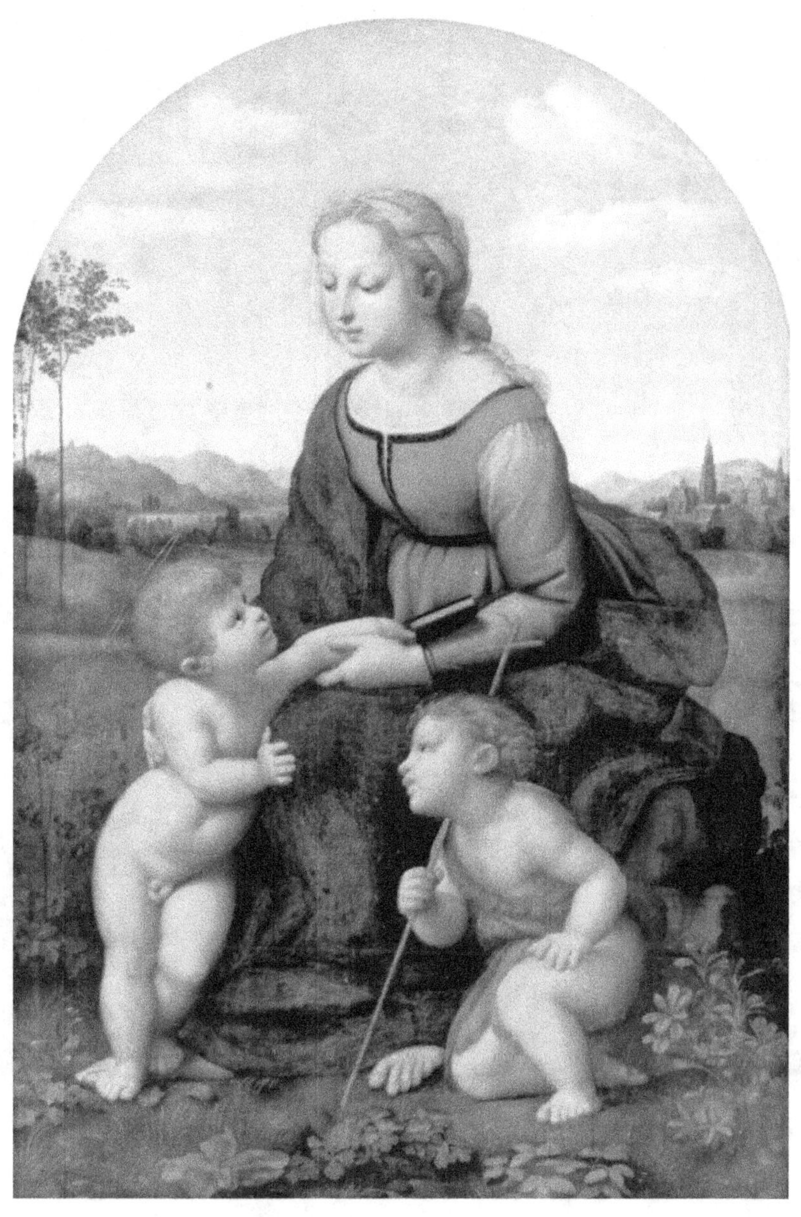

Raphael, La Belle Jardiniere, 1507, Louvre

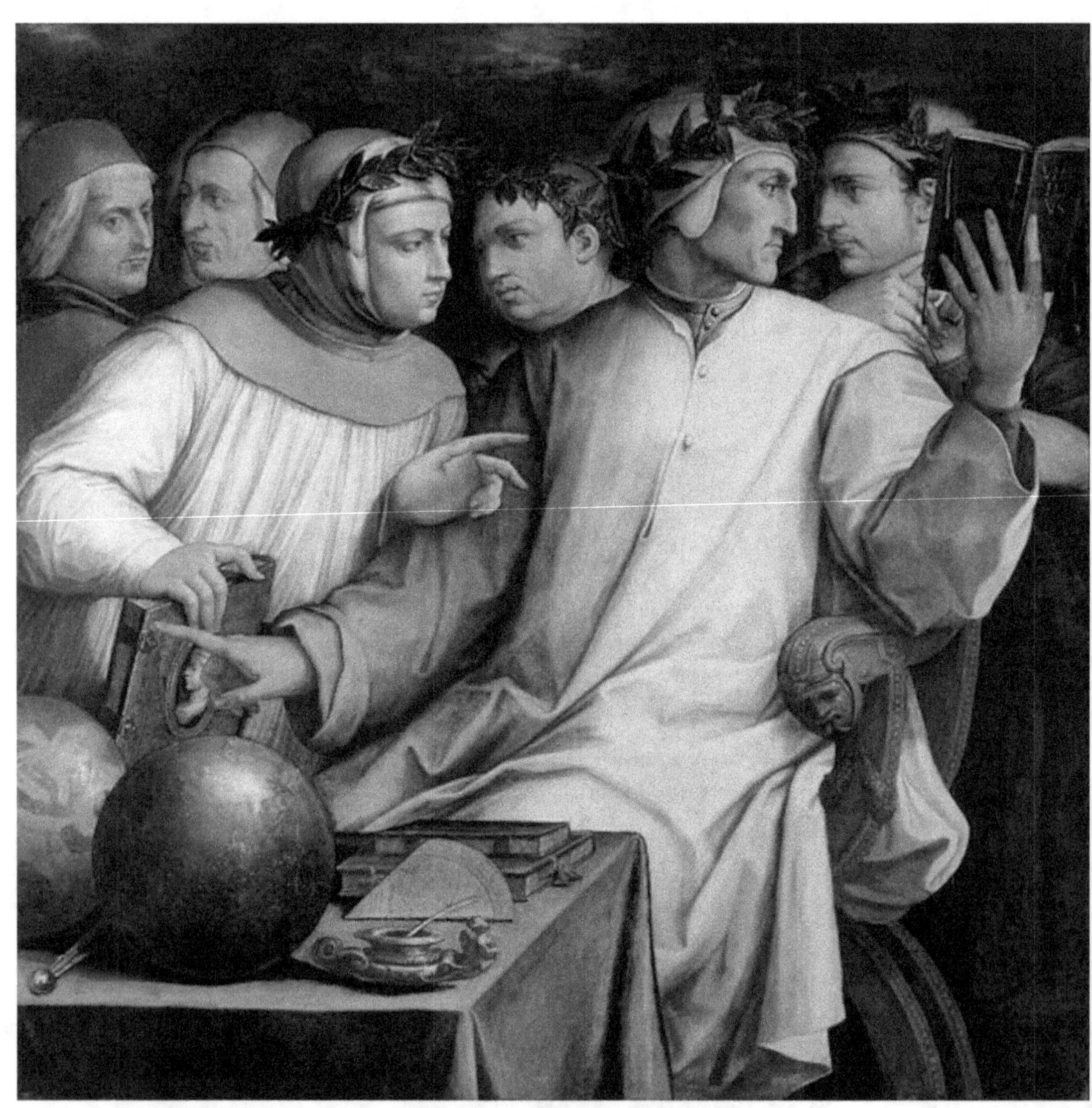

Giorgio Vasari, Six Tuscan Poets, 1544, Minneapolis

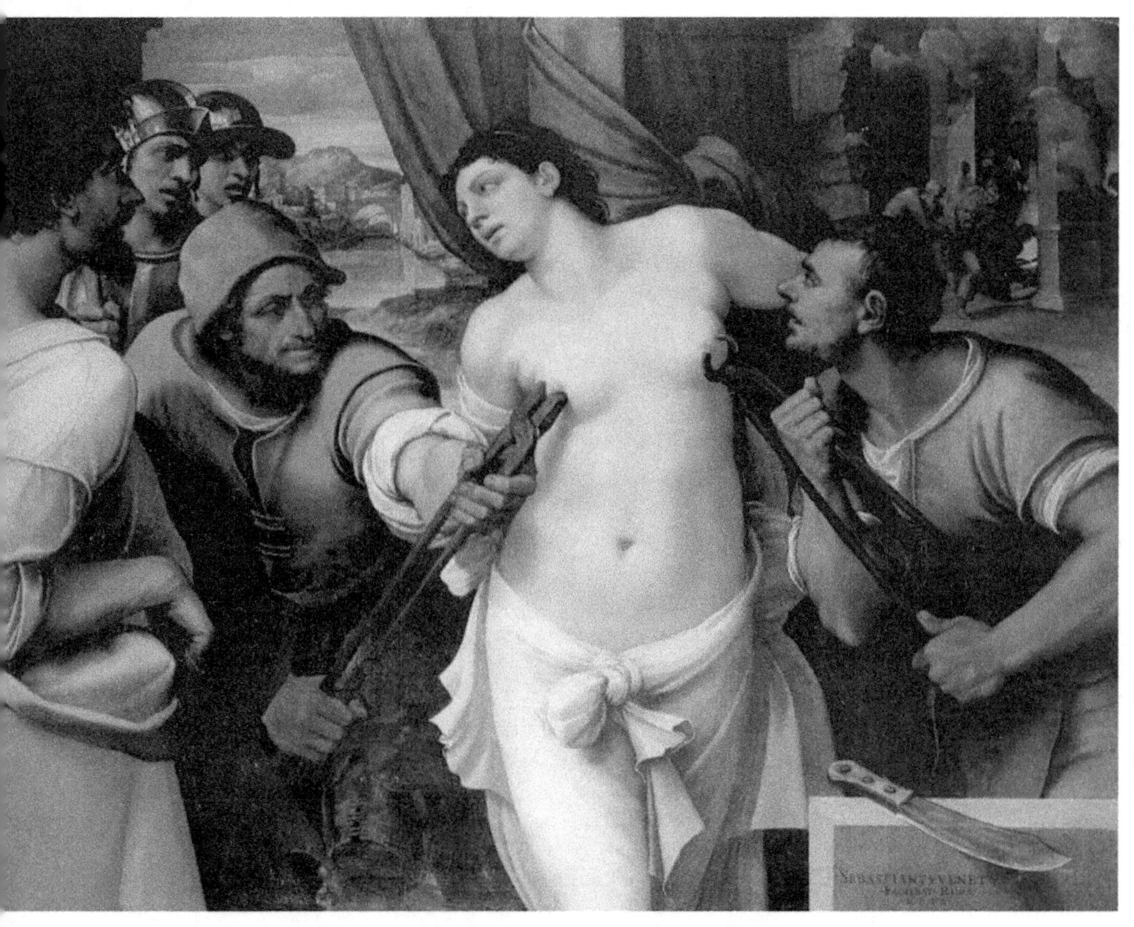

Sebastiano del Piombo, The Martyrdom of St Agatha, 1520,
Pitti Palace, Florence

MAURICE SENDAK

& the art of children's book illustration

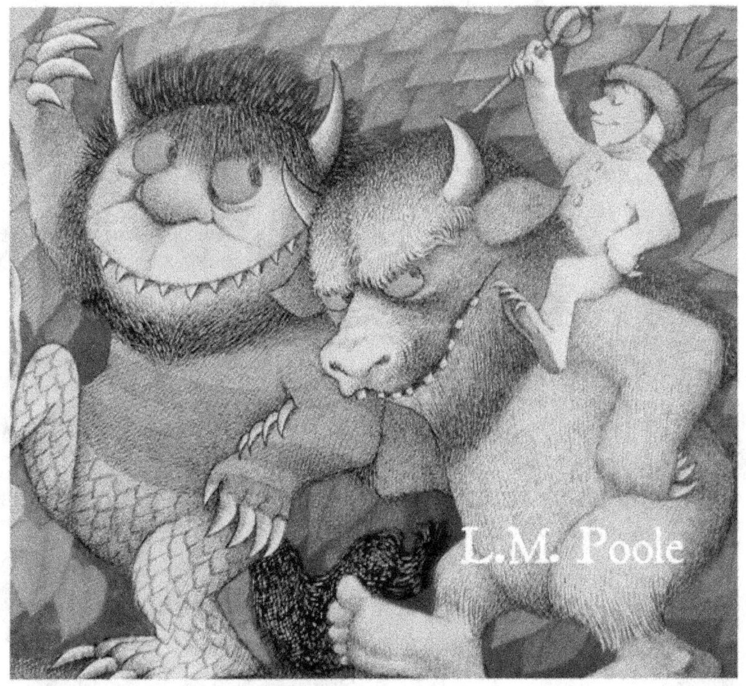

Maurice Sendak is the widely acclaimed American children's book author and illustrator. This critical study focuses on his famous trilogy, *Where the Wild Things Are, In the Night Kitchen* and *Outside Over There*, as well as the early works and Sendak's superb depictions of the Grimm Brothers' fairy tales in *The Juniper Tree*. L.M. Poole begins with a chapter on children's book illustration, in particular the treatment of fairy tales. Sendak's work is situated within the history of children's book illustration, and he is compared with many contemporary authors.

Fully illustrated. The book has been revised and updated for this edition.
ISBN 9781861714282 Pbk   ISBN 9781861713469 Hbk

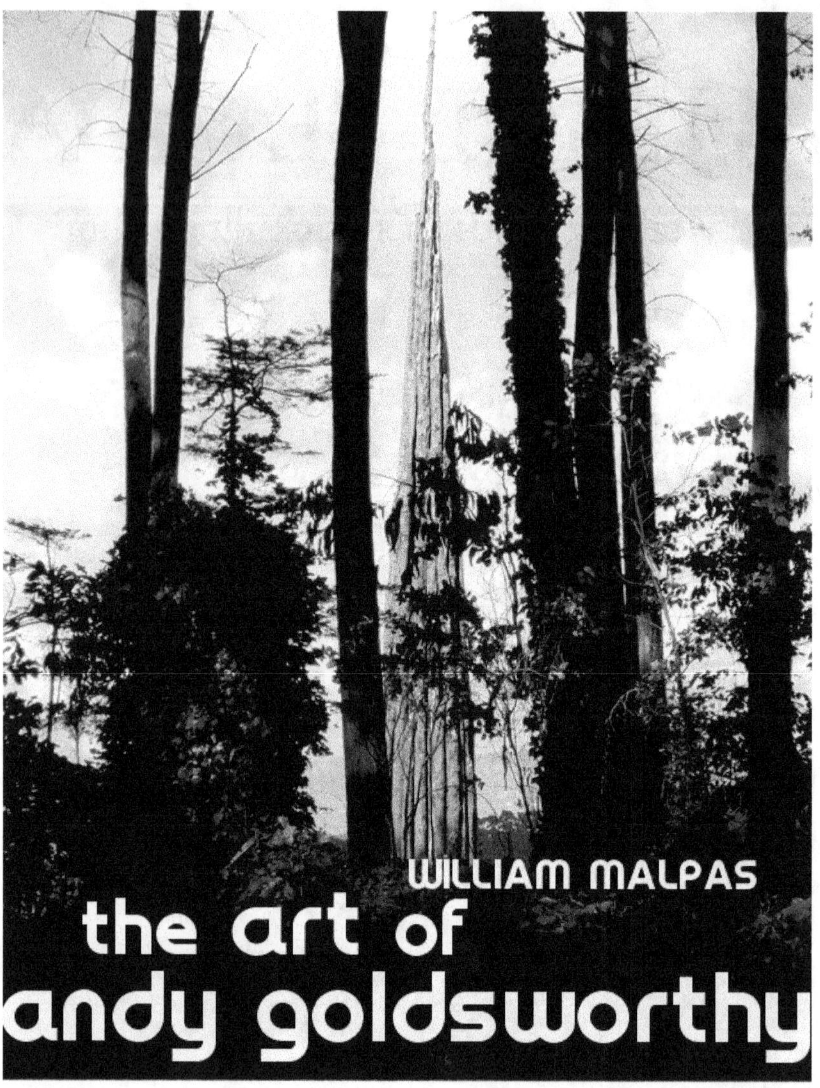

This is the most comprehensive and detailed account of the art of Andy Goldsworthy available.

This study of Andy Goldsworthy discusses all of Goldsworthy's major exhibitions, books and projects, including the *Sheepfolds* project; *Garden of Stones* in New York; TV and dance collaborations; and the books *Wood, Stone, Time* and *Passage*. William Malpas surveys all of Goldsworthy's output, and analyzes his relation with other land artists such as Robert Smithson, the Christos, Walter de Maria, Chris Drury, Richard Long and David Nash; women sculptors; sculpture in the modern era; and Goldsworthy's place in the contemporary British art scene.

The book has been updated and revised for this new edition.

ISBN 9781861714107 Pbk   ISBN 9781861714114 Hbk
Fully illustrated   www.crmoon.com

Beauties, Beasts, and Enchantment

CLASSIC FRENCH FAIRY TALES

Translated and with an Introduction
by Jack Zipes

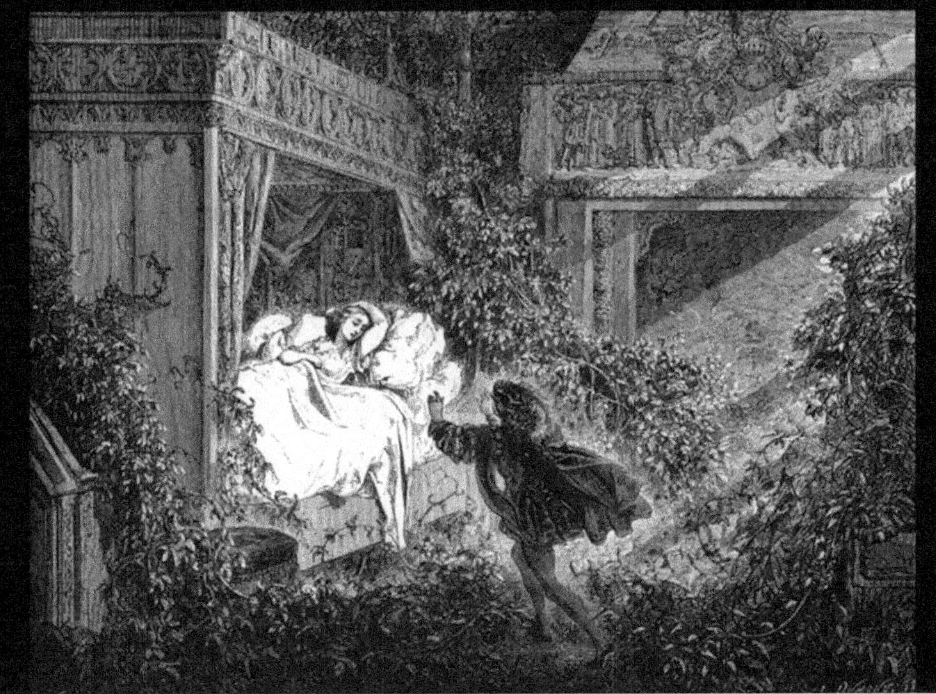

A collection of 36 classic French fairy tales translated by renowned writer Jack Zipes.
Cinderella, Beauty and the Beast, Sleeping Beauty and *Little Red Riding Hood* are among the
classic fairy tales in this amazing book.
Includes illustrations from fairy tale collections.
Jack Zipes has written and published widely on fairy tales.

'Terrific... a succulent array of 17th and 18th century 'salon' fairy tales'
- *The New York Times Book Review*

'These tales are adventurous, thrilling in a way fairy tales are meant to be... The translation
from the French is modern, happily free of archaic and hyperbolic language... a fine and
sophisticated collection' - *New York Tribune*

'Enjoyable to read... a unique collection of French regional folklore' - *Library Journal*

'Charming stories accompanied by attractive pen-and-ink drawings' - *Chattanooga Times*

Introduction and illustrations   612pp.   ISBN 9781861712510 Pbk   ISBN 9781861713193 Hbk

CRESCENT MOON PUBLISHING

web: www.crmoon.com e-mail: cresmopub@yahoo.co.uk

ARTS, PAINTING, SCULPTURE

The Art of Andy Goldsworthy
Andy Goldsworthy: Touching Nature
Andy Goldsworthy in Close-Up
Andy Goldsworthy: Pocket Guide
Andy Goldsworthy In America
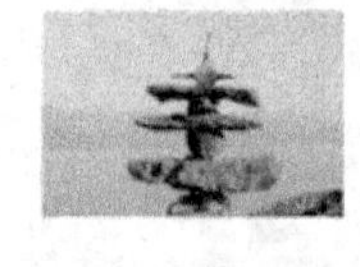
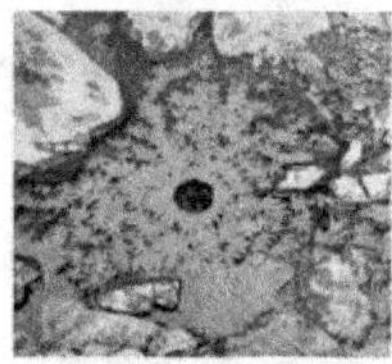
Land Art: A Complete Guide
The Art of Richard Long
Richard Long: Pocket Guide
Land Art In the UK
Land Art in Close-Up
Land Art In the U.S.A.
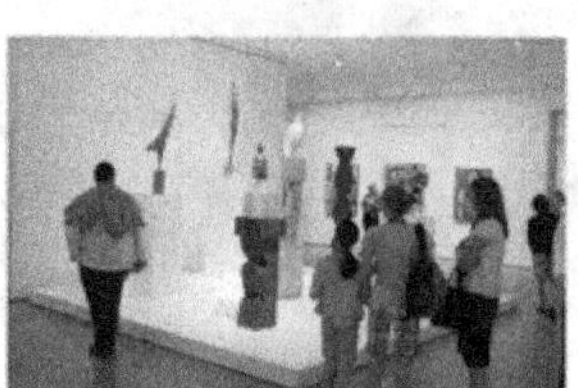
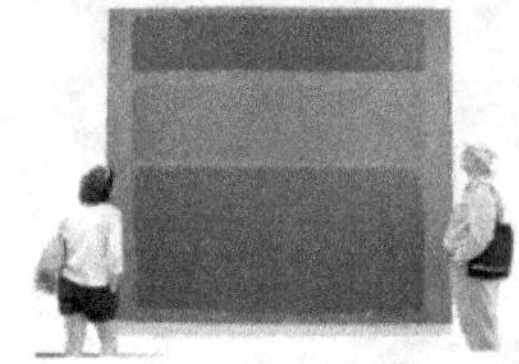
Land Art: Pocket Guide
Installation Art in Close-Up
Minimal Art and Artists In the 1960s and After
Colourfield Painting
Land Art DVD, TV documentary
Andy Goldsworthy DVD, TV documentary
The Erotic Object: Sexuality in Sculpture From Prehistory to the Present Day
Sex in Art: Pornography and Pleasure in Painting and Sculpture
Postwar Art
Sacred Gardens: The Garden in Myth, Religion and Art
Glorification: Religious Abstraction in Renaissance and 20th Century Art
Early Netherlandish Painting
Leonardo da Vinci
Piero della Francesca
Giovanni Bellini
Fra Angelico: Art and Religion in the Renaissance
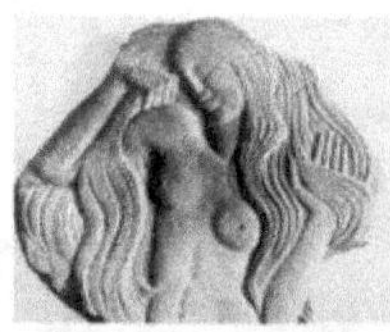
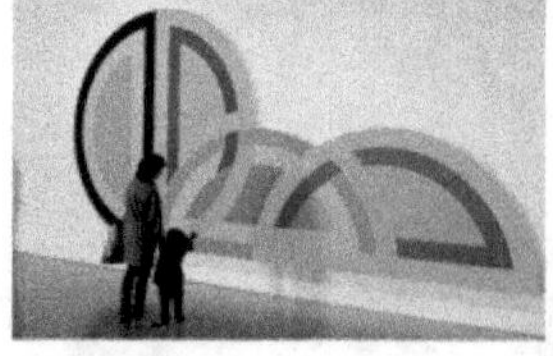
Mark Rothko: The Art of Transcendence
Frank Stella: American Abstract Artist
Jasper Johns
Brice Marden
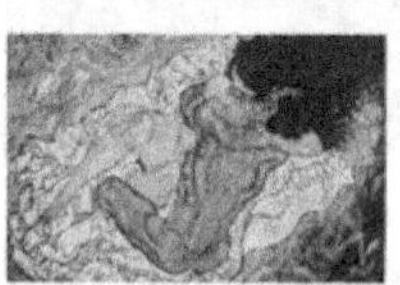
Alison Wilding: The Embrace of Sculpture
Vincent van Gogh: Visionary Landscapes
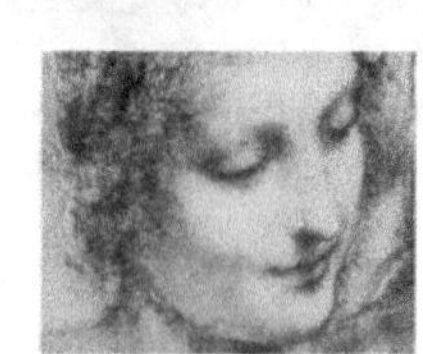
Eric Gill: Nuptials of God
Constantin Brancusi: Sculpting the Essence of Things
Max Beckmann
Caravaggio
Gustave Moreau
Egon Schiele: Sex and Death In Purple Stockings
Delizioso Fotografico Fervore: Works In Process 1
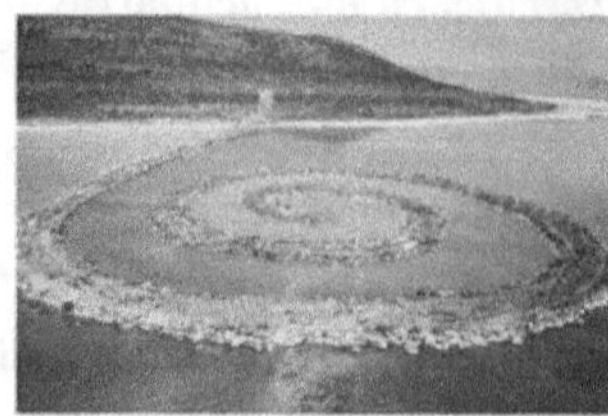
Sacro Cuore: Works In Process 2
The Light Eternal: J.M.W. Turner
The Madonna Glorified: Karen Arthurs

LITERATURE

J.R.R. Tolkien: The Books, The Films, The Whole Cultural Phenomenon
J.R.R. Tolkien: Pocket Guide
Tolkien's Heroic Quest
The *Earthsea* Books of Ursula Le Guin
Beauties, Beasts and Enchantment: Classic French Fairy Tales
German Popular Stories by the Brothers Grimm
Philip Pullman and *His Dark Materials*
Sexing Hardy: Thomas Hardy and Feminism
Thomas Hardy's *Tess of the d'Urbervilles*
Thomas Hardy's *Jude the Obscure*
Thomas Hardy: The Tragic Novels
Love and Tragedy: Thomas Hardy
The Poetry of Landscape in Hardy
Wessex Revisited: Thomas Hardy and John Cowper Powys
Wolfgang Iser: Essays and Interviews
Petrarch, Dante and the Troubadours
Maurice Sendak and the Art of Children's Book Illustration
Andrea Dworkin
Cixous, Irigaray, Kristeva: The *Jouissance* of French Feminism
Julia Kristeva: Art, Love, Melancholy, Philosophy, Semiotics and Psychoanalysis
Hélene Cixous I Love You: The *Jouissance* of Writing
Luce Irigaray: Lips, Kissing, and the Politics of Sexual Difference
Peter Redgrove: Here Comes the Flood
Peter Redgrove: Sex-Magic-Poetry-Cornwall
Lawrence Durrell: Between Love and Death, East and West
Love, Culture & Poetry: Lawrence Durrell
Cavafy: Anatomy of a Soul
German Romantic Poetry: Goethe, Novalis, Heine, Hölderlin
Feminism and Shakespeare
Shakespeare: Love, Poetry & Magic
The Passion of D.H. Lawrence
D.H. Lawrence: Symbolic Landscapes
D.H. Lawrence: Infinite Sensual Violence
Rimbaud: Arthur Rimbaud and the Magic of Poetry
The Ecstasies of John Cowper Powys
Sensualism and Mythology: The Wessex Novels of John Cowper Powys
Amorous Life: John Cowper Powys and the Manifestation of Affectivity (H.W. Fawkner)
Postmodern Powys: New Essays on John Cowper Powys (Joe Boulter)
Rethinking Powys: Critical Essays on John Cowper Powys
Paul Bowles & Bernardo Bertolucci
Rainer Maria Rilke
Joseph Conrad: *Heart of Darkness*
In the Dim Void: Samuel Beckett
Samuel Beckett Goes into the Silence
André Gide: Fiction and Fervour
Jackie Collins and the Blockbuster Novel
Blinded By Her Light: The Love-Poetry of Robert Graves
The Passion of Colours: Travels In Mediterranean Lands
Poetic Forms

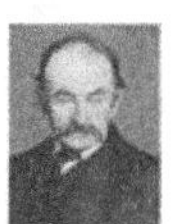
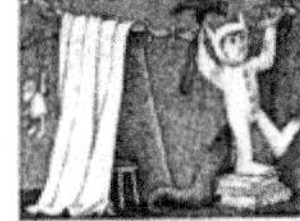
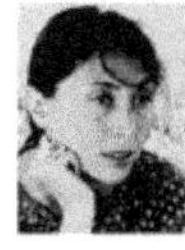
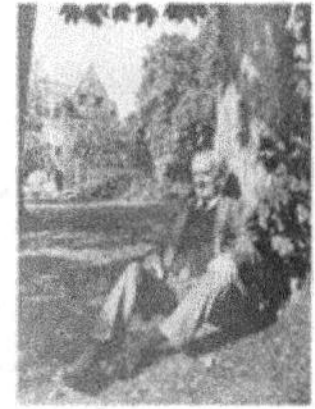
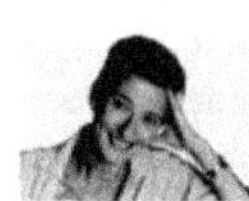
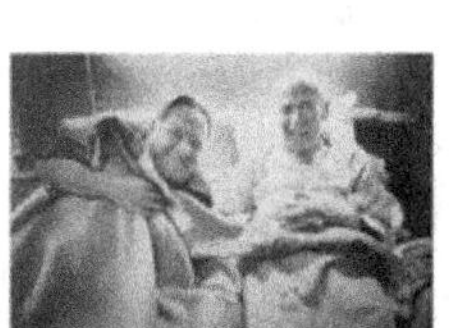
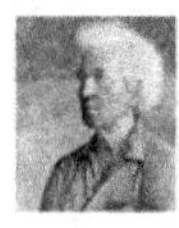
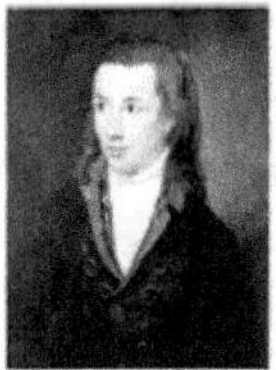

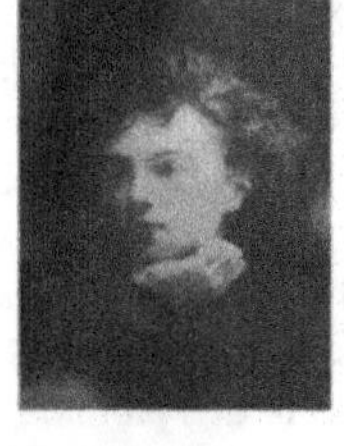
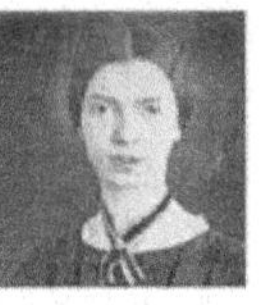
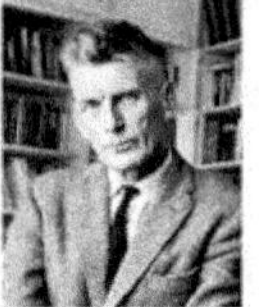
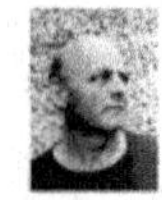
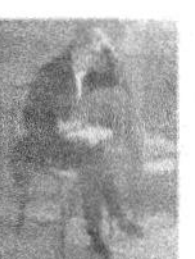
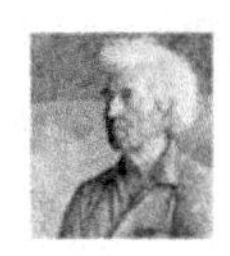
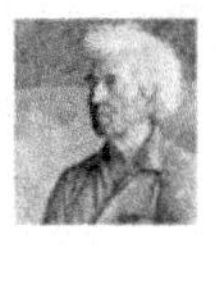
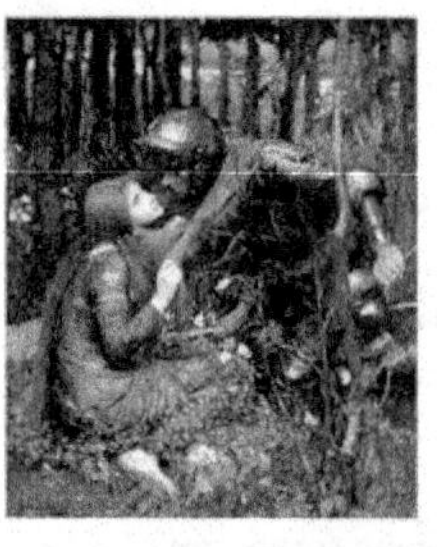
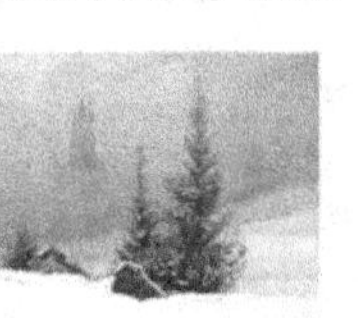
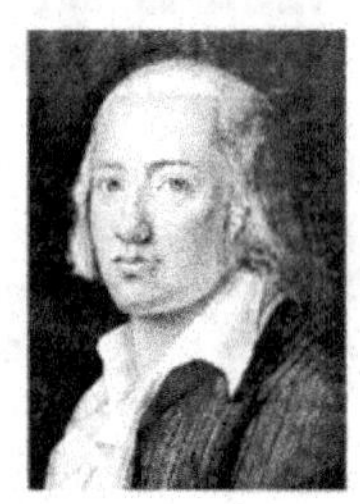
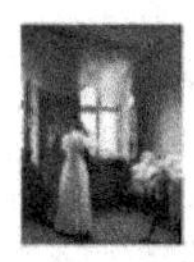
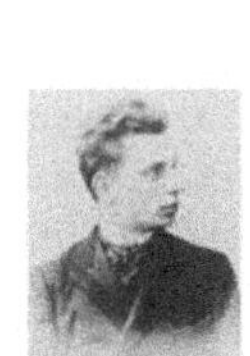
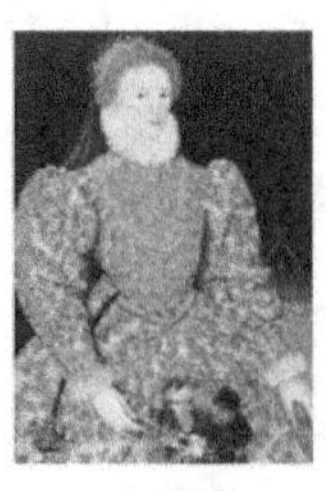

MEDIA, CINEMA, FEMINISM and CULTURAL STUDIES

J.R.R. Tolkien: The Books, The Films, The Whole Cultural Phenomenon
J.R.R. Tolkien: Pocket Guide
The *Lord of the Rings* Movies: Pocket Guide
The Cinema of Hayao Miyazaki
Hayao Miyazaki: *Princess Mononoke*: Pocket Movie Guide
Hayao Miyazaki: *Spirited Away*: Pocket Movie Guide
Tim Burton : Hallowe'en For Hollywood
Ken Russell
Ken Russell: *Tommy*: Pocket Movie Guide
The Ghost Dance: The Origins of Religion
The Peyote Cult
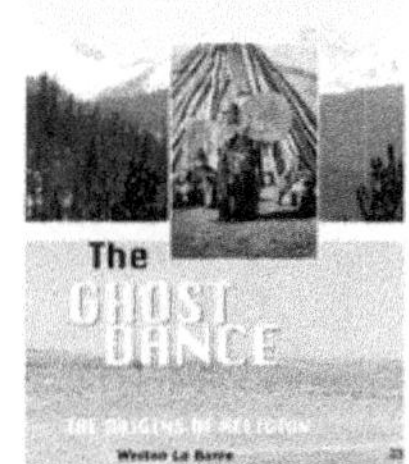
Cixous, Irigaray, Kristeva: The *Jouissance* of French Feminism
Julia Kristeva: Art, Love, Melancholy, Philosophy, Semiotics and Psychoanalysis
Luce Irigaray: Lips, Kissing, and the Politics of Sexual Difference
Hélène Cixous I Love You: The *Jouissance* of Writing
Andrea Dworkin
'Cosmo Woman': The World of Women's Magazines
Women in Pop Music
HomeGround: The Kate Bush Anthology
Discovering the Goddess (Geoffrey Ashe)
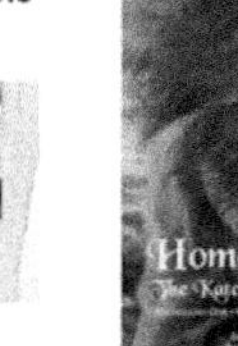
The Poetry of Cinema
The Sacred Cinema of Andrei Tarkovsky
Andrei Tarkovsky: Pocket Guide
Andrei Tarkovsky: *Mirror*: Pocket Movie Guide
Andrei Tarkovsky: *The Sacrifice*: Pocket Movie Guide
Walerian Borowczyk: Cinema of Erotic Dreams
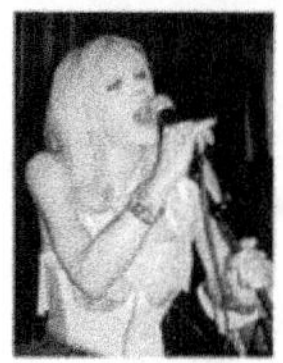
Jean-Luc Godard: The Passion of Cinema
Jean-Luc Godard: *Hail Mary*: Pocket Movie Guide
Jean-Luc Godard: *Contempt*: Pocket Movie Guide
Jean-Luc Godard: *Pierrot le Fou*: Pocket Movie Guide
John Hughes and Eighties Cinema
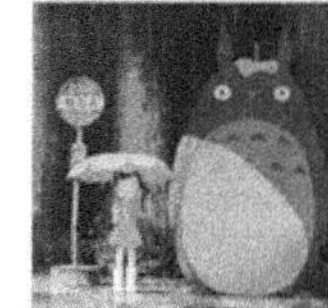
Ferris Bueller's Day Off: Pocket Movie Guide
Jean-Luc Godard: Pocket Guide
The Cinema of Richard Linklater
Liv Tyler: Star In Ascendance
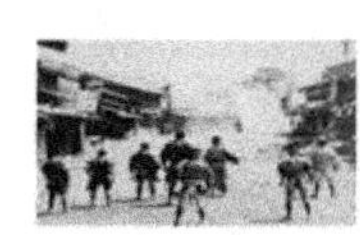
Blade Runner and the Films of Philip K. Dick
Paul Bowles and Bernardo Bertolucci
Media Hell: Radio, TV and the Press
An Open Letter to the BBC
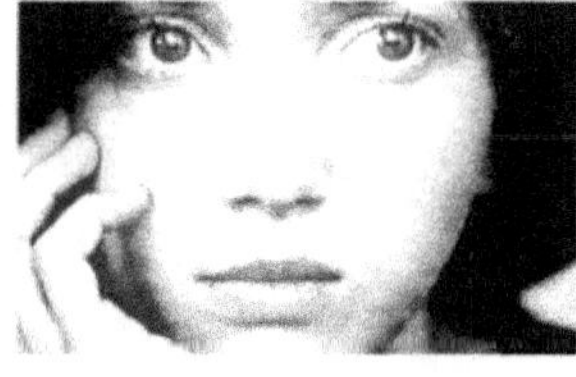
Detonation Britain: Nuclear War in the UK
Feminism and Shakespeare
Wild Zones: Pornography, Art and Feminism
Sex in Art: Pornography and Pleasure in Painting and Sculpture
Sexing Hardy: Thomas Hardy and Feminism

The Light Eternal is a model monograph, an exemplary job. The subject matter of the book is beautifully organised and dead on beam. (Lawrence Durrell)
It is amazing for me to see my work treated with such passion and respect. (Andrea Dworkin)

CRESCENT MOON PUBLISHING
P.O. Box 1312, Maidstone, Kent, ME14 5XU, Great Britain. www.crmoon.com

cresmopub@yahoo.co.uk   www.crescentmoon.org.uk